American STRE★MLINE

BERNARD HARTLEY & PETER VINEY
CONNECTIONS

An intensive American English course
for intermediate students
Student's Edition

American adaptation by Flamm/Northam Authors and Publishers Services, Inc.

Oxford University Press

Oxford University Press

200 Madison Avenue New York, N.Y. 10016 USA

Walton Street Oxford OX2 6DP England

OXFORD is a trademark of Oxford University Press.

© B. Hartley, P. Viney,
and Oxford University Press 1983

First published 1983
Printing (last digit): 20 19 18 17 16 15 14 13 12

Library of Congress Cataloging in Publication Data

Hartley, Bernard.
American streamline connections.

   "American adaptation by Flamm/Northam Authors
and Publishers Services, Inc."
   Includes index. 1. English language—Text-books for
foreign speakers. 2. English language—United States.
I. Viney, Peter.—II. Title.
PE1128.H368—1983—428.2'4—83-13504
ISBN 0-19-434115-1 (student's ed.)
ISBN 0-19-434116-X (teacher's ed.)
ISBN 0-19-434119-4 (cassette)

Illustrations by:

Marla Frazee	Paddy Mounter
Julian Graddon	Andrew Mudryk
Paul Harvey	Beverly Pardee
Alun Hood	Gary Rees
Pete Kelly	Elly Robinson
Edward McLachlan	Bill Sanderson
Yoshi Miyake	Brian Sweet
Brian Moore	Ken Thompson

Photographs by:

Simon Baigelman	Terry Williams
Vernon Brooke	

*The publishers would like to thank the following for their
time and assistance:*
Bonne Cleaners, Ltd., The Chemist Shop, Inc.,
Deak and Perera, Fifth Ave./New York, Eastern Air-
lines, Gimbels/New York, G.P. Putnam Publishing
Co., Hair Inn, Jasmine, La Rousse, New York Bus
Service, Optical Exchange, Public Information
Department/Lincoln Center, Inc., Radio Shack, Fifth
Avenue, Record Explosion, Stonybrook Market
Store, Union Tours, Inc., United States Park Police

*The publishers would like to thank the following for per-
mission to reproduce photographs:*
All-Sport Photographic Ltd., Pat Brindley, Photo-
graphic Department, B.L. Cars, Cowley, British
Petroleum Co. Ltd., Colour Library International
Ltd., Colorific Photo Library, Colorsport, Gerry
Cranham, Mary Evans Picture Library, Alan Hutch-
ison Library, Keystone Press Agency Ltd., London
Features International Ltd., The Mansell Collection,
New York Convention & Visitors Bureau, Inc., *N.Y.
Daily News*, Paul Popper Ltd., Syndication Interna-
tional Ltd., The Times Newspapers Ltd., United
Press International

Printed in Hong Kong

Students can buy cassettes which
contain a recording of the texts
and conversations in this book.

1 All Aboard!

The *Sun King* is a cruise ship. It is sailing around the Caribbean. There are a lot of tourists on the ship. Most of them are from the United States, but some of them are from Canada and South America. It's the seventh day of the cruise, and their ship is sailing from Venezuela to Barbados. All of the passengers and most of the crew are on deck for the captain's party.

A: Hello. My name's Pierre Lafontaine. I'm from Montreal.
B: Hi. I'm Heather Hillman.
A: Where do you come from?
B: I come from Montgomery.
A: Montgomery. Where's that?
B: It's in Alabama. Have you heard of Alabama?
A: Oh, yes, Alabama. It's in the South. I've never been to the South.

Questions

What is the *Sun King*?
What is the *Sun King* doing?
Are all of the passengers American?
Ask, "How many of them . . . ?"
Where are the others from?
Is it the first day of the cruise?
Ask, "Which day?"
Where's the ship?
Where are the passengers?
Why are they there?

C: What an awful party!
D: Oh, really? Do you think so?
C: Yes, I do. Oh, by the way, my name's
   Marianne Wilson.
D: I'm Tom Gray. Nice to meet you.
C: I work in a bank. What do you do?
D: Well, I'm captain of this ship. It's my party.
C: Oh, I'm so sorry!
D: That's O.K. No problem.

E: Would you like another drink?
F: What?
E: Would you like another drink?
F: Oh, yes, please. I'd like some orange juice.
E: With ice?
F: No, thanks.

Exercise 1

THE SUN KING	BOARDING CARD	
Last Name	First Name	Middle Initial
Nationality	Date of Birth	Occupation
Address		Phone
Signature		Date

All of the passengers had to fill out this card.
Here are some of the questions:
What's your last name?
What's your first name?
What's your middle initial?
When were you born?
What nationality are you?
What do you do?
Where do you live?
Ask somebody these questions and fill out the
card for them.

Exercise 2

This is a first-class cabin on the *Sun King.* There
are two beds, and there's a shower. . . . Describe
the cabin.

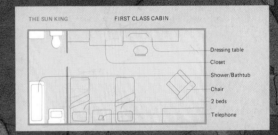

THE SUN KING   FIRST CLASS CABIN

Dressing table
Closet
Shower/Bathtub
Chair
2 beds
Telephone

Exercise 3

Itinerary

Day of the week	Day of the cruise	Location
Saturday	1st	Miami
Monday	3rd	Jamaica
Wednesday	5th	Curaçao
Thursday	6th	Venezuela
Saturday	8th	Barbados
Sunday	9th	Martinique
Monday	10th	Virgin Islands
Tuesday	11th	Dominican Republic
Thursday	13th	Haiti
Saturday	15th	Miami

Where have they been? When did they go there?
Where haven't they been yet?
Where are they going? When are they going there?

2 Using the telephone

A: Operator. Can I help you?
B: What's the area code for San Francisco?
A: 415.
B: Thank you. Now, let's see. 1-415-555-1212.
C: Directory Assistance for which city?
B: San Francisco.
C: Can I help you?
B: Alta California Co. at 1414 Adrian Street.
C: The number is 692-1285.
B: Thank you.
C: You're welcome. Have a nice day.

San Francisco
(415) 692-1285
Alta California Co.
1414 Adrian Street

Miami
(305) 947-8976
Pamela Kramer
62 Palm Road

Chicago
(312) 288-6656
Helen Ching
1254 Sunset Blvd.

Boston
(617)924-3050
William Good
118 Fairview Avenue

D: Perry, Ross, and Company. Can I help you?
E: I'd like to speak to James Singh, please.
D: Which department is he in?
E: Accounting.
D: Just a moment. I'll connect you. It's ringing.

James Singh
Accounting

Anita Palacios
Advertising

Pat Williston
Sales

Angel Lopez
Marketing

F: Let's see. I dial "0" first: 0-314-725-5735.
G: Operator.
F: Hello. This is a collect call, Operator.
G: What's your name?
F: Joan Sinewski.
G: Can you spell that, please?
F: S-I-N-E-W-S-K-I.
G: Just a moment, please.
F: Thank you.

Joan Sinewski
Laura Nazarian
Arthur Katzenback
Kathy Fitzgerald
Pamela McQueen
Victor Bendix

H: Who are you talking to?
I: Nobody.
H: Well, why are you holding the phone?
I: My watch stopped. I'm calling the time. Listen. (Good morning. At the tone the time will be 9:52 and 40 seconds—*Beep.*)
H: What number is the time?
I: 976-1616.

New York Phone Services
The Time: 976-1616
The Weather: 976-1212.
Sports News: 976-1313
Cultural News: 976-2323

3 Fizz is fantastic!

Brian Humble: Meet Mrs. Edna Lopez of San Antonio, Texas. Mrs. Lopez has three young children, and she has to do a lot of wash. There are two piles of dirty clothes on this table. With this pile Mrs. Lopez is going to use new "Fizz," and with that pile she's going to use another leading detergent. We have two identical washing machines here, Mrs. Lopez. The only difference is "Fizz." While the machines are working, let's have some coffee.

Brian: O.K., both machines have stopped, and Mrs. Lopez has taken the clothes out. Well, Mrs. Lopez, what do you think?
Mrs. L.: Well, I've washed these clothes in "Fizz" and those clothes in the other detergent.
Brian: Can you see any difference?
Mrs. L.: I sure can! These clothes are much cleaner. And they're whiter and softer than the others.
Brian: These clothes? You washed these clothes with new "Fizz"!
Mrs. L.: That's right, Brian. It's really much better than my usual detergent. My clothes have never been cleaner than this!
Brian: So, which detergent are you going to use from now on?
Mrs. L.: New "Fizz," of course. It's the best detergent I've ever used!

is best at the laundromat too!

A lot of people don't have washing machines. They do their wash at a laundromat.

Instructions:

1 Measure "Fizz" into the machine.
2 Load clothes into the machine. Don't overload.
3 Select water temperature—hot, warm, or cold.
4 Insert three quarters in the coin slot.
5 Clothes are ready in 30 minutes.

Exercise

While you're waiting at the laundromat, you can have a cup of coffee. Write instructions for the coffee machine.

4 Olympic Update

It's time now for our "Olympic Update." Our report is coming live by satellite from the Olympic Games. Here's our reporter, Pat Sweeney.

This is the Olympic swimming pool, at the center of the Olympic complex. The most important event today was certainly the women's 200-meter freestyle competition. An American, Doris Kennedy, was first and won the gold medal. She swam the 200 meters in a new world's record of 1 minute 58 seconds. The United States won two gold medals yesterday and three the day before, so in the first three days of the Olympic Games the American team has won six gold medals.

Javelin

Here you see Jack Lumber from Canada. This morning he won the men's javelin final. On his first try he threw the javelin over 100 meters. Nobody has ever done that before—a new world's record. Unfortunately, there was nearly a terrible accident in the javelin event. Harry Jones, the American competitor, slipped when he was throwing his javelin, and it hit a judge in the foot. Luckily, the judge was fine.

Gymnastics

Here we are in the Olympic Gymnasium. Olga Ivanov, the fifteen-year-old Russian gymnast, has just finished her routine. We're waiting for the results now.

And here they are! She has an average of 9.5 points. That's the best score today! Olga's won the gold medal.

Exercise 1

Here are some Olympic records.
Men's Javelin Throw: Miklos Nemeth, Hungary—Montreal, 1976—310 ft. 4 in.
Miklos Nemeth, a Hungarian, won the men's javelin throw in Montreal in 1976. He threw it 310 feet 4 inches.

Women's Swimming (800-meter freestyle): Michelle Ford, Australia—Moscow, 1980— 8 min. 28.9 sec.
Michelle Ford, an Australian, won the women's 800-meter freestyle in Moscow in 1980. She swam 800 meters in 8 minutes 28.9 seconds.

Write sentences for:
Men's 800-Meter Run: Alberto Juantorena, Cuba—Montreal, 1976—1 min. 43.5 sec.
Men's Swimming (100-meter butterfly): Mark Spitz, United States—Munich, 1972—54.27 sec.
Women's High Jump: Sara Simeoni, Italy— Moscow, 1980—6 ft. 5½ in.
Men's Long Jump: Bob Beamon, United States—Mexico City, 1968—29 ft. 2½ in.
Women's Javelin Throw: Maria Colon, Cuba—Moscow, 1980—224 ft. 5 in.
Women's Swimming (100-meter butterfly): Kornelia Ender, East Germany—Montreal, 1976—1 min. 0.13 sec.

High jump

We're waiting for the last jumper. Ted Kelly from England is going to jump. The bar is at 2.30 meters.

Now he's beginning his last try.

And he's jumped!

Oooh! He's crashed into the bar!

He's landing. The bar's fallen. Is he hurt?

No, no, he's all right. He's getting up and walking away, but he's a very disappointed man.

Exercise 2

A He's going to lift it.   **B** He's lifting it.   **C** He's lifted it.

Write sentences:

A • • • jump.   **B** • • •   **C** • • •

A • • • throw.   **B** • • •   **C** • • •

5 I'll be there

A: Psst! He'll be here tomorrow night.
B: Will he? What time?
A: Eight o'clock sharp.
B: Will he be at the train station?
A: No, he'll be at the airport. He'll be on Pan Am Flight 207.
B: Will he be alone?
A: No, he won't. He'll be with his wife.
B: Will you be there?
A: Yes. I'll be outside in the white station wagon.
B: What about the money?
A: Don't worry. It'll be there.
B: O.K. I'll see you tomorrow night.

Exercise

A He'll be here tomorrow.
B *He won't be here tomorrow.*
C *Will he be here tomorrow?*

A They'll be there next week.
B . . . .
C . . . .

A . . . .
B She won't be here next Monday.
C . . . .

A . . . .
B . . . .
C Will you be here next year?

6 Monday morning

David: What's the matter, honey?
Sue: Oh, I don't know.
David: Come on, something's the matter. What is it?
Sue: It's just life. It's so boring!
David: It's not that bad. You have the children.
Sue: But Kim will be at school and Josh's only a baby! It's all right for you. You'll leave in five minutes, but I'll be here all day. You won't be home till seven!
David: One of us has to work, honey.
Sue: Yes, dear, but your day will be interesting. My day will be the same as every other day.
David: My work isn't always interesting.
Sue: I know, but you travel around, you meet different people, and you do different things. Who will *I* meet today? What will *I* do? Huh? Oh, I'll do the dishes, feed the baby, wash the clothes, clean the house, give the baby a bath, walk the dog . . .
David: But . . . but . . . honey. . . .
Sue: Then I'll go to the supermarket, pick Kim up at school, make dinner, pick you up at the station, eat dinner, do the dishes again. . . .
David: But . . . but . . . honey . . .
Sue: Then I'll feed the baby again and put the kids to bed. What a life! Today, tomorrow, this week, next week, this month, next month, next year—forever!
David: It's just Monday morning, honey. You'll feel O.K. tomorrow.
Sue: Will I?

His Monday
David Shaw, television news reporter
 8:30 catch the train
 9:30 arrive at the MBS studio
10:00 tape an interview with Miss Universe
12:00 have lunch with movie producer
 3:00 interview Paul McCartney at Kennedy Airport
 5:00 meet Walter for drinks
 6:00 catch the train
 7:30 have dinner
 8:30 watch TV
 9:30 walk the dog
11:00 go to bed

Her Monday
Sue Shaw, housewife
 8:15 drive David to the train station
 8:45 wash the dishes
10:00 feed the baby
10:30 do the wash
12:00 clean the house
 2:30 go to the supermarket
 3:00 pick Kim up at school
 4:00 make dinner
 6:45 meet David at the station
 7:30 have dinner
 8:30 wash the dishes
 9:00 feed the baby
10:15 go to bed

Exercise 1
What will he do at 8:30?
He'll catch the train.
Write questions and answers about David.

Exercise 2
When will she drive David to the train station?
She'll drive David to the train station at 8:15.
Write questions and answers about Sue.

7 Rafael Calderon del Castillo

Rafael Calderon del Castillo is the Secretary-General of the United Nations. He's one of the busiest men in the world. He's just arrived at the New Delhi airport. The Indian Prime Minister is meeting him. Later they'll talk about problems in Asia.

Yesterday he was in Moscow. He visited the Kremlin and had lunch with Soviet leaders. During lunch they discussed the international political situation.

Tomorrow he'll fly to Nairobi. He'll meet the President of Kenya and other African leaders. He'll be there for twelve hours.

The day after tomorrow he'll be in London. He'll meet the British Prime Minister, and they'll talk about European economic problems.

Next weekend he'll be back in New York at the United Nations. Next Monday he'll speak to the General Assembly about his tour. Then he'll need a few days to rest.

Questions

Who is Rafael Calderon del Castillo?
Where's he just arrived?
Who's meeting him?
What'll they talk about?

Where was he yesterday?
Who did he have lunch with?
What did they discuss?
When did he leave Moscow?

Where will he fly tomorrow?
Who will he meet?
How long will he be there?

When will he be in London?
Who will he meet?
What will they talk about?

Where will he be next weekend?
What will he do on Monday?
Why will he need a rest?

Most people need eight hours of sleep.

1 How many hours do you need?
2 How many hours did you sleep last night?
3 Did you sleep well or badly?
4 Are you tired today?
5 What time do you usually go to bed?
6 What about last night?
7 What time do you usually get up?
8 What about this morning?

Some people use
a) sleeping pills
b) warm milk
c) electric blankets

1 Do you use   **a b c ?**
2 Have you ever used **a b c ?**
3 Why did you use **a b c ?**
4 Last night did you use **a b c ?**

Some people sleep on their
a) backs
b) sides
c) stomachs

1 How do you sleep?
2 Do you change positions?

SLEEP AND DREAMS

Some people can sleep
a) on a train
b) on a plane
c) on a bus
d) in a car
e) in a chair
f) standing up

1 Can you sleep   **a b c d e f ?**
2 Have you ever slept **a b c d e f ?**
3 When? Where?

Some people
a) snore
b) walk in their sleep
c) talk in their sleep

1 Do you | snore?
     | walk in your sleep?
     | talk in your sleep?
2 Have you ever snored?
Have you ever walked/talked in your sleep?
3 How do you know?

Everybody dreams every night.

1 Do you dream in black and white or color?
2 Do you always/sometimes/rarely remember your dreams?
3 Have you ever had a nightmare?
4 Have you ever had a dream about falling/flying/running/dying?
5 Have you ever had the same dream again? How often?

9 At the drugstore

A: Can I help you?
B: Yes, thank you. I have a terrible headache.
A: How long have you had it?
B: About two or three hours.
A: Well, try these pills Take two every four hours.
B: Thank you very much.

headache
stomachache
backache
earache
sore throat

pills
capsules
tablets
drops
throat lozenges

C: Good morning. Can I help you?
D: Good morning. I'd like a toothbrush, please.
C: Electric?
D: No, just a regular toothbrush.
C: Nylon or natural bristles?
D: Nylon, please.
C: Hard, soft, or medium?
D: Soft. My dentist says soft is best.
C: What color would you like?
D: It doesn't really matter. Oh, white's O.K.

white
blue
red
green
yellow
pink

E: Could I have a tube of toothpaste, please?
F: With fluoride or without?
E: With.
F: Will that be all?
E: Yes, thank you. I only have a twenty-dollar bill.
F: That's all right. Here's your change.

a tube of toothpaste
  with fluoride/without
a bar of soap
  large/small
a pack of razor blades
  five/ten
a bottle of mouthwash
  large/small
a can of spray deodorant
  large/small
a roll of film
  35 mm/126/110
a box of throat lozenges
  large/small

G: Could you fill this prescription, please?
H: Sure. Do you want to wait?
G: How long will it take?
H: It'll be ready in about twenty minutes.
G: Oh. I'll come back later.
H: All right. I'll have it here for you.
G: Should I pay now or later?
H: Later will be fine.

about twenty minutes
a few minutes
a moment
about an hour
half an hour

10 The Chairman of the Board

Thomas B. Worthington III is the Chairman of the Board of Directors of Texxo Corporation. Howard is his typist; Sylvia, his administrative assistant; and Laura, his private secretary.

TBW III: Come in!
Howard: Yes, Mr. Worthington?
TBW III: No, no, Howard. I don't want you right now.
Howard: Who did you want, Mr. Worthington?
TBW III: I want Sylvia. I want her immediately.
Howard: I'll go and find her.

TBW III: Come in.
Sylvia: Did you want to see me, Mr. Worthington?
TBW III: Yes, Sylvia. I wanted to see you ten minutes ago.
Sylvia: I'm sorry. I was meeting with Blum in the accounting department.
TBW III: You can manage things this afternoon. I want a company limousine at two o'clock.
Sylvia: All right. Do you want the Cadillac or the Continental?
TBW III: Hmm. The Cadillac. Something's wrong with the phone in the Continental.
Sylvia: Where do you want to go?
TBW III: The Pan Am terminal at Kennedy Airport. I want to meet Maggie Silver from Dallas. She wants to buy Texxo!
Sylvia: Maggie Silver, the multimillionaire? Wow! Uh—anything else?
TBW III: No, that's all, Sylvia. I want to see Laura now.

TBW III: Laura, come in.
Laura: You want to see me?
TBW III: Yes, yes. I want to eat lunch in my office today. Call the Executive Dining Room. I want my usual lunch—salad and fish.
Laura: What time?
TBW III: Twelve-thirty. Oh, and I want you to reserve a table at Lutece for eight o'clock. I'll take Maggie Silver.
Laura: Lutece at eight. All right.
TBW III: And I want Howard to pick up some theater tickets for tomorrow night.
Laura: Theater tickets. Anything else?
TBW III: No, Laura. That's all—for now.

Exercise 1

I wanted to do something.
What did you want to do?
1 They wanted to go somewhere.
2 He wanted to buy something.
3 We wanted to meet someone.
4 She wanted to eat something.
5 I wanted to see someone.

Exercise 2

He/her/make dinner.
He *wants* her *to* make dinner.

1 She/me/reserve a table.
2 I/him/help me.
3 They/her/clean the room.
4 My parents/me/learn English.
5 The police/them/stop.
6 She/me/dance.
7 The teacher/us/do our homework.

Exercise 3

When I was young, my father wanted me to be a doctor. He wanted me to work hard.

What did your | father / mother / teachers | want you to do?

What did you want to do?

11 Look, feel, taste, sound, smell

A: I like your fur coat, Helen.
B: Oh, you do? Thank you.
A: Yes, it looks very expensive
B: Really? It wasn't expensive. I got it at a secondhand store.
A: You did? It doesn't look secondhand. It looks brand new.

C: Brrr! It feels cold in here.
D: It does?
C: Yes, really cold. Is the heat on?
D: Yes, it is. It'll feel warmer in a minute.

E: Waiter!
F: Yes, sir.
E: These vegetables aren't fresh!
F: But they *are* fresh, sir.
E: Well, they don't taste fresh to me.

G: Listen to my new stereo, Eduardo. Does it sound all right?
H: Yes, it sounds fine to me.
G: I think the bass is too loud.
H: No, it sounds perfect. It sounds better than mine.

I: Have you changed your perfume?
J: Yes, why? Do you like it?
I: Yes, it smells terrific. What is it?
J: It's "Rosalie" by Devlon.
I: It smells expensive. Is it?
J: I don't know. It was a present.
I: A present? Who gave you perfume?
J: Jennifer. My friend Jennifer.

12 A science fiction story

The spaceship flew around the new planet several times. The planet was blue and green. They couldn't see the surface of the planet because there were too many white clouds. Then the spaceship descended slowly through the clouds and landed in the middle of a green forest. The two astronauts put on their space suits, opened the door, climbed carefully down the ladder, and stepped onto the planet.

The woman looked at a small control unit on her arm. "It's O.K.," she said to the man. "We can breathe the air. It's a mixture of oxygen and nitrogen." Both of them took off their helmets and breathed deeply.

They looked at everything carefully. All the plants and animals looked new and strange. They couldn't find any intelligent life.

After several hours, they returned to their spaceship. Everything looked normal. The man turned on the controls, but nothing happened. "Something's wrong," he said. "I don't understand. The engines aren't working." He switched on the computer, but that didn't work either. "Eve," he said, "we're stuck here. We can't take off!"

"Don't worry, Adam," she replied. "They'll rescue us soon."

13 It's too hot!

In the hotel coffee shop (7:30 p.m.)

Mike: Come on, Kim. Hurry up! Drink your coffee. We have to catch a taxi to the airport. We'll be late.

Kim: I can't hurry. This coffee's too hot for me to drink.

Mike: Why don't you put some ice in it?

Kim: Ice? I don't want ice in my coffee. Oh, O.K., O.K.

Mike: There! Is it cool enough for you to drink now?

Kim: Yes, but it tastes awful!

At the airport (8:00 p.m.)

Kim: Oh, no! The Delta counter looks a mile away! Oh, well, let's go. Let's get the luggage.

Mike: Wow! What did you put in these suitcases? Rocks?

Kim: Only clothes. Why? Are they heavy?

Mike: Yes, they are.

Kim: The taxi driver managed to carry them.

Mike: Well, they're too heavy for me to carry.

Kim: Well, I'm not strong enough to help you. Porter, over here, please.

On the plane (9:00 p.m.)

Kim: Oh, Mike. I didn't tell you. My sister called yesterday. You were at the convention.

Mike: Oh? Which one? Tiffany?

Kim: Yes. She had some news. She wants to get married.

Mike: Married! She isn't old enough to get married. She's only seventeen. Who does she want to marry?

Kim: Marc McIntosh.

Mike: Marc McIntosh! I can't believe it! He's too old for her. He's over 40!

Kim: I know, but she loves him.

At their destination (11:00 p.m.)

Kim: Oh, no! There goes the last bus!

Mike: Well, let's walk to the highway and catch a different bus.

Kim: It's a mile away! That's too far for me to walk. Let's catch a taxi.

Mike: Another taxi! My name isn't Rockefeller! We aren't rich enough to go everywhere by taxi.

Kim: Mike, haven't you forgotten something?

Mike: What?

Kim: We have three suitcases. Do you really want to walk?

Mike: You're right. Taxi!

IN THE HOTEL COFFEE SHOP

AT THE AIRPORT

ON THE PLANE

AT THEIR DESTINATION

Exercise 1

He can't lift it. It's very heavy.
It's too heavy for him to lift.

1 They can't drink it. It's very hot.
2 She can't buy it. It's too expensive.
3 He can't answer it. It's very hard.
4 We can't see it. It's very small.

Exercise 2

Can he lift the boxes?
No, he isn't strong enough to lift them.

1 Can you touch the ceiling? (tall)
2 Can they buy that house? (rich)
3 Can he understand the questions? (smart)
4 Can that cat catch the bird? (quick)

14 A phone call

Vicki: Hello?

Randy: Vicki? Is that you?

Vicki: Yes, uh huh. Who's this?

Randy: It's Randy.

Vicki: Randy? Randy who?

Randy: What do you mean, "Randy who?" Randy Dixon, of course.

Vicki: Oh, Randy, I'm sorry.

Randy: Yes. We had a date last night. Where were you? I waited for two hours.

Vicki: Oh, I'm sorry, Randy. I couldn't come.

Randy: Couldn't come! Why not?

Vicki: Well, I had to wash my hair.

Randy: Wash your hair! Why didn't you call me?

Vicki: I wanted to call you, but—uh—I—uh—couldn't remember your phone number.

Randy: It's in the phone book.

Vicki: Yes, of course, but—uh—I couldn't remember your last name.

Randy: Oh. But why did you have to wash your hair last night?

Vicki: Well, I had to do it last night because I'm going to the theater tonight.

Randy: The theater! Who with?

Vicki: George. George McQueen, my boss's son.

Randy: I see.

Vicki: He asked me yesterday, and I couldn't say no.

Questions

Who's calling?
Who's answering the phone?
Did they have a date?
Ask, "When?"
Why couldn't she come?
Did she want to call him?
Why didn't she call him?
Is his number in the phone book?
Why couldn't she find it?
Did she have to wash her hair?
Ask, "Why?"
Is she going to the theater with Randy?
Ask, "Who . . . with?"
When did he ask her?
Why did she say yes?

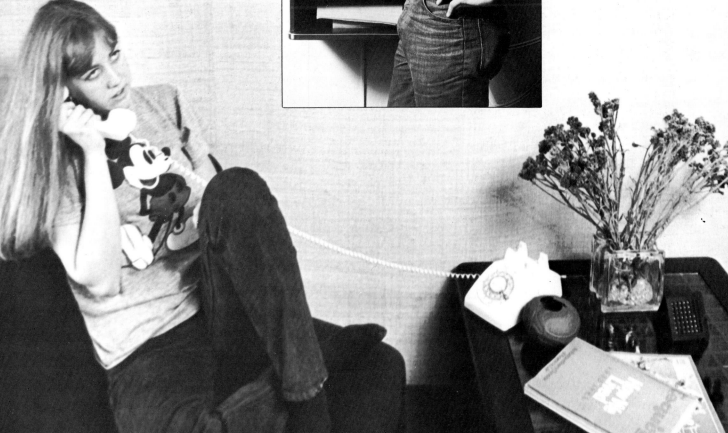

15 Army Recruiting Office

Sergeant: Good morning. Are you the new janitor of the building?

Corona: Janitor? No, I'm not. I want to join the army.

Sergeant: What! You! In the army?

Corona: Yes. I want to be a soldier. This is the Army Recruiting Office, isn't it?

Sergeant: Well—uh—yes. Sit down, son.

Corona: Thanks.

Sergeant: Now, why do you want to be a soldier, Mr. . . . uh—what's your name, son?

Corona: Corona. Frankie Corona. Well, I saw the commercial on TV last night. It looked nice. Vacations, money, travel, education, pension. . .

Sergeant: I see. Yes, it's a good life in the army.

Corona: Terrific!

Sergeant: Now, do you have any questions?

Corona: Let's see. Yes. Will I have to get a haircut?

Sergeant: Oh yes, you'll have to get a haircut—and wear a uniform.

Corona: A uniform!

Sergeant: Oh yes, and you'll have to obey orders. But you won't have to clean latrines.

Corona: What are latrines?

Sergeant: Toilets. I've never had to clean toilets.

Corona: What about the work? Will I have to work hard?

Sergeant: Oh yes. You'll have to work hard. But hard work pays off, you know.

Corona: Hmm. And what about education?

Sergeant: Oh, yes. There are a lot of opportunities. Maybe you'll be a computer programmer or a communications expert one day.

Corona: O.K. I'd like to join.

Sergeant: All right. Just sign here, Frankie.

Corona: There you are—Frankie Corona.

Sergeant: Corona!

Corona: Huh?

Sergeant: Stand up. Stand up straight, Corona. Now, march! Left, right, left, right. You're in the army now!

Exercise

A friend is going into the army in your country.
What will he have to do?
What won't he have to do?

Write six sentences.

16 Smokequitters

Most smokers want to quit smoking. Smoking is very dangerous to your health. Some people quit without any trouble. Other people need help. Smokequitters is an organization of ex-smokers. They help smokers quit smoking. They give special courses. The first day they ask questions. Here are some of the questions:

1 How long have you been a smoker?
2 How many cigarettes do you smoke every day?
3 Can you remember your first cigarette?
4 Have you ever been able to quit for a short time?
5 Why do you want to quit?

Here are some of the results:

Richard York has smoked for thirty years. He smokes two packs of cigarettes a day. He can't remember his first cigarette. He's never been able to quit—even when he's been sick. Poor Richard has heart problems now. He has to quit or he'll die.

Sue Shaw has been a smoker for nine years. She smokes a pack a day. She can remember her first cigarette. She got sick. She has been able to quit twice—once when she was expecting her baby, Josh, and the other time when she had a bad sore throat. She wants to live longer and look better, so she wants to quit smoking.

Joyce Ducas started smoking when she was sixteen. She has smoked for twelve years. She can remember her first cigarette. It tasted terrible. She has never been able to quit. Her husband doesn't like the taste of cigarettes. He has never been able to kiss her. She wants to kiss her husband, and she wants to be healthy.

Exercise

Richard York/not quit.
Richard York *hasn't been able* to quit.

Write sentences
Some people/get help at Smokequitters.
Sue Shaw/quit two times.
Joyce Ducas/not quit/twelve years.
Mr. Ducas/not kiss his wife.

17 Changes

School owner: Why do you want to study computer programming?

Robbie Evans: Well, I lost my job last month, and I haven't been able to find another one.

School owner: I see. Do you have any money?

Robbie Evans: I have some money, and my girlfriend will be able to help me.

School owner: Good. The course costs $750.

Robbie Evans: Whew! Will I be able to find a job as a computer programmer?

School owner: Oh sure! You'll be able to get a good job and make lots of money. Please sign here.

Home owner: This is the room, Miss Vann. Do you like it?

Lois Vann: It's very nice. Is it quiet? I'm a writer.

Home owner: You'll be able to work with no problem. There's almost no noise here.

Lois Vann: Will I be able to use the kitchen?

Home owner: Yes, of course.

Lois Vann: Fine. It looks good. (*Crash!*) What's that?

Home owner: Oh, that's just our neighbor. He works on old cars. (*Crash!*) He's usually quiet.

Personnel Manager: Come in and have a seat, Jim. You work in the mail room, right?

Jim Worsinger: Yeah, that's right. I want to transfer to the International Sales Division.

Personnel Manager: Why do you want to join the International Division, Jim?

Jim Worsinger: Well, I don't really. I just want to go to Africa or Latin America.

Personnel Manager: Hmm. What qualifications do you have?

Jim Worsinger: Qualifications? I've never been able to learn Spanish—or anything else!

Personnel Manager: Well, what will you be able to do in the International Sales Division?

Jim Worsinger: I don't know. But I won't be able to work very hard. I have a bad back.

Look at this

He'll be able to find a job.
He won't be able to work hard.
Will she be able to use the kitchen?

Exercise

Complete this conversation using *be able to find.*

Applicant: I want to teach English in South America. . . . a job in Bogotá?

Interviewer: Did you graduate from college?

Applicant: Oh, yes. I have a master's degree in ESL.

Interviewer: Then . . . a job at our Bogotá center.

Applicant: What about living arrangements? . . . an apartment?

Interviewer: Well, that's hard. . . . (not) . . . an apartment right away, but . . . one after a few months.

18 Checks, money, and credit cards

A: Next! Good morning.
B: Good morning. I'd like to cash this check, please.
A: O.K. $100. Oh! You haven't signed it.
B: Really? Oh, I'm sorry. Here you are.
A: Thank you. How would you like the money?
B: Four twenties and two tens, please.

$100 (4 × $20/2 × $10)
$50 (5 × $10)
$200 (5 × $20/20 × $5)
$35 (1 × $20/1 × $10/5 × $1)

C: I'd like to change these English pounds, please.
D: O.K. How many pounds do you have?
C: Thirty. What's the exchange rate?
D: Just a second, I'll check today's rates.

English
 pounds (30)
German
 marks (50)
Japanese
 yen (5000)
Argentinian
 pesos (200)
Swiss
 francs (70)

E: I'd like to get this, but I don't have enough cash on me. Do you take traveler's checks?
F: Yes, of course.
E: Good. Here you are.
F: Thank you. I'll need some identification too.
E: Sure. Is my driver's license all right?
F: Yes, that's fine.

traveler's checks
 driver's license
American Express
 student I.D. card
Visa
 passport
Master Card
 faculty I.D. card

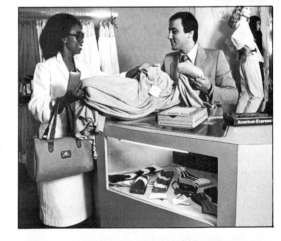

G: Hello. Can I help you?
H: Thank you. My name is Toshiko Akiyama. I'm expecting a transfer from my bank in Tokyo.
G: By mail or telegram?
H: By telegram.
G: Let me see. Here it is. Akiyama, $500 from the Fuji Bank in Tokyo. Do you have your driver's license with you?
H: No, but I have my passport. Will that be all right?
G: Your passport? I'll have to check with an officer.

Toshiko Akiyama/
 $500/Fuji Bank/Tokyo

Linnea Costa da
 Silva/$300/Banco do
 Brasil/Rio de Janeiro

Monique Duplantie/
 $1000/Banque de
 Montreal/Quebec

Juan Enrique
 Botero/$3000/Banco
 Colombiano/Bogotá

19 Excursion trip to Egypt

Mr. Harris: I looked through these brochures last night. I'd like to make a reservation for the excursion to Alexandria leaving July 16.

Travel Agent: The Cleopatra Hotel or the King Tut Palace?

Mr. Harris: The Cleopatra. How far is it from the hotel to the beach?

Travel Agent: About a two-minute walk.

Mr. Harris: Good. How hot is it in Egypt in July?

Travel Agent: About 82°.

Mr. Harris: That's Fahrenheit of course!

Guide: And that is the Great Pyramid.

Mr. Harris: Oh, yes. It looks very high!

Guide: It's about 137 meters high. That's 450 feet.

Mr. Harris: How long are the sides?

Guide: They're 230 meters long—755 feet.

Mr. Harris: Incredible! How old is it?

Guide: It's almost four-and-a-half thousand years old.

Sailor: We're going through the Suez Canal now.

Mr. Harris: Hmm. It doesn't look very wide. How wide is it?

Sailor: About 60 meters. It's 160 kilometers long.

Mr. Harris: Really? This is a big ship. How deep is the canal?

Sailor: The average depth is about 10 meters.

Mr. Harris: Can you tell me all that in feet and miles?

Guide: Hello, Mr. Harris. Are you coming on the bus trip to Cairo tomorrow?

Mr. Harris: Oh, yes. How far is it?

Guide: It's about 150 kilometers.

Mr. Harris: How far is it in miles?

Guide: About 90, Mr. Harris.

Mr. Harris: Oh, I see. How long will it take to get there—in hours?

Guide: Three hours, Mr. Harris. I'll see you tomorrow.

	Miami	Key West	Palm Beach	Orlando	Tampa	Daytona Beach	Tallahassee
Miami		160	74	232	261	258	480
Key West	160		223	390	399	415	637
Palm Beach	74	223		170	203	197	427
Orlando	232	390	170		84	54	260
Tampa	261	399	203	84		153	245
Daytona Beach	258	415	197	54	153		239
Tallahassee	480	637	427	260	245	239	

Exercise 1

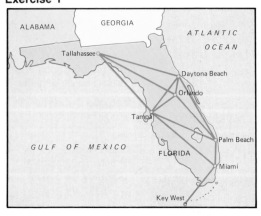

How far is it from Miami to Key West?
It's 160 miles.
Write seven sentences like this.

Exercise 2

Maria
height: 1 m 62 cm/
5 ft. 4 in.
age: 30

João
height: 1 m 85 cm/
6 ft. 1 in.
age: 27

How old is Maria?
She's thirty.
How tall is she?
*She's one meter sixty-two centimeters.
/ She's five four.*

Write two questions about João.

20 Comparisons

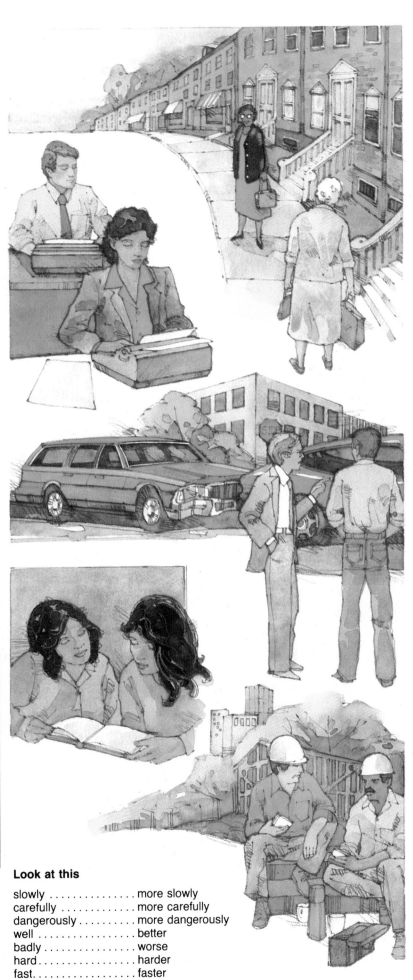

Mrs. Park and Miss Holm are retired. They live on Social Security. They go shopping every Saturday. They have to walk up a very steep hill between their apartment building and the stores. They both walk slowly. Mrs. Park always has to wait for her friend at the top of the hill because Miss Holm walks more slowly than Mrs. Park.

Anna and Rick work in the same office. They're both good typists because they type carefully. Anna never makes a mistake, and Rick rarely makes a mistake. Anna types more carefully than Rick.

Some drivers occasionally have accidents, but Alan and David are very careless drivers. Alan has already had two accidents this year, and David has had a lot more. David drives even more carelessly than Alan.

Both Gabriela and Pilar are good students. They speak English well, but Pilar has spent a year in the United States, so she speaks English better than Gabriela.

The Grayson College *Eagles* and the Redwood College *Tigers* are both near the bottom of the Western Division in college basketball. The season is nearly finished, and the *Eagles* have won only two games. They have played very badly. The *Tigers* haven't even won one game. The *Tigers* have played even worse than the *Eagles*.

BASKETBALL RATINGS
WESTERN DIVISION

Rank	College	Won	Lost
27	Napa State "Pirates"	8	10
28	North Dakota "Lions"	5	12
29	Grayson "Eagles"	2	15
30	Redwood "Tigers"	0	16

Tony and Jim work for a construction company. They're very hard workers. They work about twelve hours a day. Tony often works on weekends. He makes more money than Jim because he works harder than Jim.

Look at this

slowly	more slowly
carefully	more carefully
dangerously	more dangerously
well	better
badly	worse
hard	harder
fast	faster

21 A day off

Al Bellini works for an import-export company in Los Angeles. One morning last summer, Al called his office at nine o'clock. His boss, Ralph Vasquez, answered the phone.

Ralph: Hello. Ralph Vasquez.
Al: Hello, Ralph. This is Al Bellini.
Ralph: Oh, hi, Al. What's up?
Al: I don't think I can come to work today, Ralph.
Ralph: Oh? What's the problem?
Al: I've got a very bad sore throat.
Ralph: Yes, you sound sick.
Al: Yes. I'll stay in bed today, but I'll be able to come tomorrow.
Ralph: That's all right, Al. Stay in bed until you feel well enough to come to work.
Al: Thank you, Ralph. Good-bye.
Ralph: Bye, Al.

Ralph liked Al a lot. At 12:30 he got into his car, drove to a store, and bought some fruit for him. He went to Al's apartment and rang the doorbell. Al's wife, Stella, answered the door.

Stella: Oh, Ralph! Hello! Come in. How are you?
Ralph: Fine, thanks, Stella. I've come to see Al. How is he?
Stella: He doesn't look very well. I wanted him to see the doctor.
Ralph: I'll go in and see him. Hi, Al!
Al: Oh! Hi. Hi, Ralph—uh—uh—have a seat.
Ralph: I've brought some fruit for you, Al.
Al: Thanks a lot, Ralph.
Ralph: Well, I had to pass near here anyway. How's your throat?
Al: It seems a little better. I'll be O.K. tomorrow.
Ralph: Good, good. Take care. Good-bye, Al.
Al: Bye, Ralph. Thanks for passing by.

At three o'clock, Ralph locked his office door and turned on his portable TV. He wanted to watch an important baseball game. It was the Atlanta Braves versus the Los Angeles Dodgers. Both teams were playing well, but neither team could score. The crowd was cheering and booing. It was very exciting.

Then at 3:20, Sam Zapata of the Dodgers hit a home run. Ralph jumped out of his chair. He was very excited. He was smiling happily when suddenly the cameraman focused on the crowd. Ralph's smile disappeared, and he looked very upset. Al Bellini's face, in close-up, was there on the screen. He didn't look sick, and he didn't sound sick. He was smiling happily and cheering wildly.

22 Applying for a job

JOB APPLICATION FORM

Job _Export sales representative_
Name _Paula Chandler_
Address _32 Johnson Road, Lowell, MA 01854_
Social Security No. _423-50-2151_

Education

	Institution	Address	Degree
High School	Emerson High School	Lowell MA	Diploma ☑ yes ☐ no ☑ BS ☐ BA major _Bus Admin_
College	Suffolk University	Boston MA	☐ MS ☐ MA ☐ PhD in ___
Graduate School			
Other	Sperry Sales Seminars	New York NY	2 Certificates

Work Experience

Employer	Address		Position
Lipton Machines	New York NY - 6 Years		Latin American Sales Rep
Computech	Stanford CT - 4 Years		Sales Rep for Mexico and Central America

Special skills _Spanish_

BMI Import-Export Corp. · Darien, Connecticut

JOB APPLICATION FORM

Job _Secretary - Export Manager's Office_
Name _Gary Alan Prator_
Address _59 Crosby Avenue, Fairfield CT 06430_
Social Security No. _036-45-9271_

Education

	Institution	Address	Degree
High School	Fairfield H.S.	Fairfield CT	Diploma ☑ yes ☐ no ☐ BS ☐ BA major ___
College			☐ MS ☐ MA ☐ PhD in ___
Graduate School			
Other			

Work Experience

Employer	Address	Position
Stanley Manufacturing Co.	Bridgeport CT - 6 months	secretary
Texxo Chemical Corp.	Bridgeport CT - 2 months	secretary
Fairfield Hospital	Fairfield CT - 1 year	secretary
Market Planners Inc.	New Haven CT - 8 months	secretary

Special skills _typing, short hand_

Art Miranda: How do you do? It's Paula Chandler, isn't it?

Paula Chandler: Yes. How do you do?

Art: Have a seat. I'm Art Miranda, and I have your application form here. I just want to check the information.

Paula: Fine, sure.

Art: You're applying for the position of export sales representative, aren't you?

Paula: Yes, I am.

Art: You aren't from Connecticut, are you?

Paula: No, I'm from Massachusetts.

Art: You got a bachelor's degree in business administration at college, didn't you?

Paula: Yes, that's right.

Art: But you didn't get a master's degree, did you?

Paula: No, I didn't. I started working when I was 22.

Art: I see. You have worked in international sales, haven't you?

Paula: Yes, I've been a sales representative in Latin America for two companies.

Art: But you haven't worked in the Middle East, have you?

Paula: No, I haven't, but I'd like to.

Art: You can't speak Arabic or French, can you?

Paula: No, but I can read and speak Spanish very well.

Art: I'm sure you can learn another language quickly, can't you?

Paula: Sure! I'd like to learn Arabic—or French.

Fill in the blanks.

Art Miranda: Come in. Have a seat. It's Gary Prator, isn't it?

Gary Prator: Yes, Gary Alan Prator.

Art: And I'm Art Miranda. Well, I've looked over your application. Can I just check the information?

Gary: Yes, of course.

Art: You're applying for a secretarial position, • • • ?

Gary: Yes, in the export manager's office.

Art: You aren't from Darien, • • • ?

Gary: No, I'm from Fairfield.

Art: You didn't go to a secretarial school, • • • ?

Gary: No, I didn't.

Art: But you learned to type in high school, • • • ?

Gary: Right.

Art: You can take shorthand, • • • ?

Gary: Yes, I studied it in high school.

Art: I see. But you can't speak any foreign languages, • • • ?

Gary: No, I can't.

Art: You've worked as a secretary for four years, • • • ?

Gary: Yes.

Art: But you haven't stayed with one company for much time, • • • ?

Gary: No, I haven't. I've worked at some awful places.

23 Four disasters

Good evening. Our program tonight is about disasters. This year there have been fires, plane crashes, earthquakes, and volcanic eruptions. All our guests tonight have survived disasters.

Hello. I'm Susan Fisher-Diaz. I live in Chicago. I was working in my office on the 28th floor of a skyscraper. I was dictating some letters to my secretary when the fire alarm rang. I rushed out to the elevator, but it wasn't working. The stairs were full of thick smoke. We couldn't go down, so we had to go up to the roof. When we got there some people were waiting calmly. Others were shouting and screaming wildly. A helicopter managed to land on the roof and rescued six of us before the roof collapsed.

My name's Linda Reed. I was on vacation at the Med Club on Patapita, a small island in the South Pacific. I was taking a nap when the volcano erupted. The noise woke me up. I looked through the window. Everybody was running toward the port. I threw on my robe and ran to the port too. I managed to get on a cruise ship. It was leaving when the lava hit the town.

Hello. I'm Ron Byrd. I'm a farmer. I was working in the field when I saw the plane. It was flying too low to get to the airport. It was coming down fast. I was driving my tractor toward my house when the plane crashed into the trees behind me. I heard a terrible explosion. When I woke up, I was lying in bed—in a hospital.

Hi. My name's Richard Ching. My wife and I were staying with friends in Santa Librada near Los Angeles. We were having dinner when the earthquake began. Everything shook. All the plates and food fell on the floor. We were picking everything up when the ceiling fell in. We were under the table and survived. We had to wait for hours before help arrived.

24 A letter from Mexico City

John lives in Cleveland, Ohio. His girlfriend, Mary, is studying Spanish in Mexico City. She's been there for five weeks. He wants to visit her in Mexico City, and he wrote to her about two weeks ago. He's just received this reply from her.

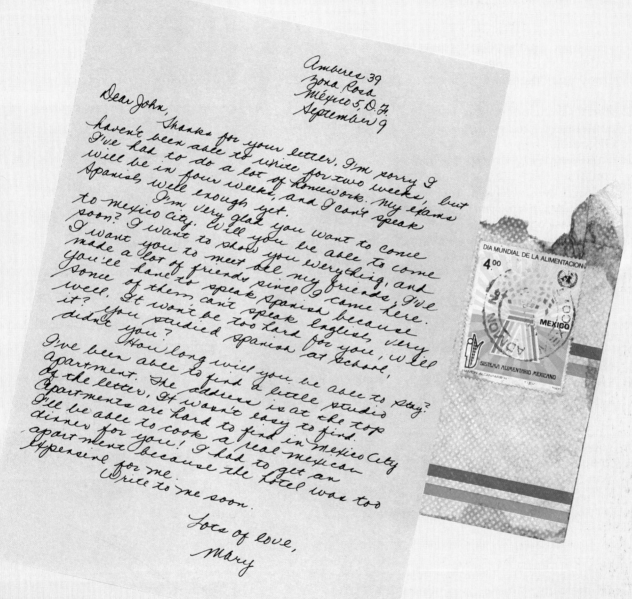

Look at this example

Thanks/letter. I/sorry/not able/write/a long time.
Thanks for your letter. I'm sorry I haven't been able to write for a long time.

Now use these words and write a letter:

Thanks/letter. I/sorry/not able/write/a long time.
I/study/every night. My test/two weeks, and I/English/yet.
I/happy/you/come/the United States. You/soon?
I/show/a lot of interesting places. I/you/meet/American friends.
I/lot/since/here.
You/English because/none (Spanish). If/too hard/you/? You/English/school/?
How long/stay? I/find/apartment.
Address/top/letter. Apartments/hard/(Los Angeles).
I/cook/American dinner/you.
I/apartment/hotel/expensive/me.

25 Traveling by air

A: Do I check in here for Eastern Flight 179 to Houston?

B: Do you already have your ticket?

A: Yes. Here you are.

B: Thank you. Can you put your luggage up here, please?

A: Sure. I have four suitcases.

B: We allow only three pieces. You'll have to pay an extra charge.

A: Oh! Can I carry this one with me?

B: No, I'm sorry. It won't fit under your seat. That's $8.00. Thank you. You can choose your seat at Gate 4. Enjoy your flight!

Eastern/Houston/four suitcases/Gate 4

Delta/New York/three suitcases and a box/ Gate 29

TWA/Chicago/two suitcases and two boxes/Gate 11

Pan Am/Detroit/three suitcases and a trunk/ Gate 3

C: (*Buzz!*) Excuse me. May I see the contents of your pockets?

A: Of course.

C: Thank you. Put everything in this container. Now go back and come through the detector again.

A: Sure. (*Buzz!*) Oh, wait! It must be my metal comb. Here it is.

C: That's fine. Put it with your other things. Now come through again.

metal comb
cigarette lighter
car keys
penknife

D: Hello. Are you going to Houston this morning?

A: Yes. I am. I'd like a window seat, please.

D: May I see your ticket?

A: Oh, sure. Here it is.

D: You want a window seat. Smoking or non-smoking?

A: Non-smoking.

D: Fine. Seat 12A. Here's your ticket and your boarding pass. Enjoy your flight!

Houston/ window seat/ non-smoking

New York/ aisle seat/ smoking

Chicago/ window seat/ smoking

Detroit/ aisle seat/ non-smoking

"Good morning, ladies and gentlemen. This is your captain speaking. I'd like to welcome you aboard Eastern's Flight 179 to Houston. We're flying at an altitude of 33,000 feet. Our speed is approximately 500 miles per hour. We'll land in Houston in two-and-a-half hours at 1:20 local time. The temperature in Houston is 78° Fahrenheit. That's 25° Celsius. In a few minutes you'll be able to see the Mississippi River on the right. Our flight attendants will serve lunch in a few minutes. Enjoy your flight!

Flight:
179
236
784

Altitude:
33,000 ft.
35,000 ft.

Speed:
500 mph
620 mph
550 mph

Temperature:
78° F/25° C
55° F/12° C
87° F/30° C

26 I've cut myself!

A: Ow! This knife's sharp! I've cut myself.
B: Let me see. Oh, you haven't cut yourself badly. It's only a scratch.
A: But I'm bleeding!
B: Don't be such a baby. It's not bleeding a lot. I'll get a Band-Aid.

C: Did you see the play on Channel 13 last night?
D: No, I didn't. What was it?
C: *Romeo and Juliet*. I cried.
D: You cried? Why?
C: Well, it was very sad. At the end, Romeo killed himself, and then Juliet killed herself.
D: It sounds dumb to me. Why did they kill themselves?
C: For love.
D: Oh! They really were dumb, weren't they?

E: My guests tonight are the rock stars, Donny and Ronny Osborne.
F: Hi, Sid. We're happy to be here.
E: You both play the guitar and sing very well. How did you learn?
F: Well, we just bought some guitars and we taught ourselves.
E: You taught yourselves—terrific!

G: I'm sorry I'm late this morning.
H: Oh, that's all right, Yolanda. It's the first time.
G: Yesterday was my first wedding anniversary.
H: Oh, congratulations, Yolanda!
G: Thanks. We went to that new restaurant on Bank Street.
H: Did you enjoy yourselves?
G: Oh, yes! We had a very good time. We had two bottles of champagne!

I: Have you seen my new microwave oven?
J: No, I haven't.
I: Oh, it's fabulous. It has an automatic timer. It can turn itself on and off. And it cleans itself!
J: Does it do windows?

Exercise

I've cut *myself.*

1 She's holding a mirror. She's looking at • • • .
2 Be careful, John! Don't hurt • • • !
3 He taught • • • to play the guitar.
4 Romeo and Juliet killed • • • .
5 We went to a party last night. We enjoyed • • • very much.
6 My cassette player is automatic. It turns • • • off.
7 They're enjoying • • • . They're on vacation.

27 Choosing a pet

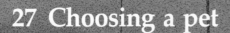

Pet store attendant: Hello. How are you today? Can I help you?

Customer: Yes. I'm looking for a pet for my son. Can you suggest anything?

Attendant: What kind of pet does he want? A traditional pet—a cat or a dog? Or something unusual?

Customer: Well, he'd like a snake or an alligator, but he isn't going to get one.

Attendant: We have a nice dog right now—a Doberman pinscher.

Customer: A Doberman pinscher! Oh no! I've heard about them on the news. They're very big and mean.

Attendant: Oh no, ma'am. They aren't as mean as some dogs.

Customer: Really?

Attendant: Yes, really. Last week we had a small dog. It was only as big as your purse, but it was as mean as the devil. It bit me three times!

Customer: Let's forget dogs then.

Attendant: What about a cat?

Customer: A cat. Hmm . . . They aren't as friendly as dogs, are they?

Attendant: No, but they don't eat as much as dogs either. And they're very clean.

Customer: Hmm. . . .

Attendant: Or what about a bird? A parrot or a parakeet. We have both.

Customer: Which do you recommend?

Attendant: Well, parakeets aren't as easy to train, and they never speak as well as parrots.

Customer: Yes, but parakeets don't need as much space as parrots, do they?

Attendant: That's true. Parakeets are very popular because they're so easy to keep.

Customer: Yes, but they're a little noisy, aren't they? I want a quiet pet.

Attendant: A quiet pet? Well, what about a goldfish? There's nothing as quiet as a goldfish.

1

Mick/Jack/strong
Mick is as strong as Jack.

Rosalie/Soul/expensive

today/yesterday/wet

the apartment building/
the church/high

this sack/that
sack/heavy

2

Her hair/his hair/long
*Her hair isn't as long
as his hair.*

portable typewriters/
office typewriters/good

English/Chinese/difficult

my writing/her
writing/clear

superhighways/country
roads/interesting

3

work hard/your boss
*Do you work as hard
as your boss?*

drive fast/Mario Andretti

type carefully/Elizabeth

speak well/the teacher

dance beautifully/Anne

4

jumbo jets/
concorde/high
*Jumbo jets don't fly as
high as concordes.*

Fred/Dan/hard

Mike/John/well

Sam/Bill/carefully

Frank/Rockie/loudly

5

Tom/drunk/wine
Robert
*Tom hasn't drunk as
much wine as Robert.*

Tom/smoked/
cigarettes/Robert
*Tom hasn't smoked as
many cigarettes as
Robert.*

the Tigers/won/
games/the Eagles

Tom/spent/money/
Robert

Ron/caught/fish/Bob

Mrs. Jones/bought/
food/Mrs. Smith

DAILY SUN

Thursday, May 5

35 cents

Vol. LVII No. 20

$15,000 BANK ROBBERY

Lone Robber Shoots Guard in Escape

NEW YORK, May 4   There was a bank robbery in the downtown financial district. Just before closing time a man entered the Wall Street branch of the Chase Manhattan Bank. He was carrying a shotgun and wearing a nylon stocking over his head. There were only a few customers in the bank at the time. He made them lie on the floor and forced a teller to put money into a sack. As he was leaving, a security guard tried to ring the alarm. The robber shot him, and the guard is now in St. Vincent's Hospital. Surgeons are trying to save his life. Last night the police arrested a man on Staten Island. The police are interrogating him.

JPOB   Detective Sergeant Angel Rodriguez had advised me of my rights under the law.
JPOB   I make this statement freely.

JPOB   Yesterday afternoon I went to the races at Belmont with my girlfriend,
JPOB   Bobbie Ann Chase. We left my apartment on Staten Island in my silver
JPOB   Corvette and drove to Belmont. We didn't stop for gas, but we got lunch
JPOB   at a fast food place. I don't remember the name of the place, but it was
JPOB   somewhere between Manhattan and Belmont. We had some hamburgers in
JPOB   the car. We arrived at the racetrack at 12:55 in time for the first race.
JPOB   We stayed there until the last race at 5 o'clock. We were very lucky. I won
JPOB   a lot of money, but I can't remember exactly how much. That's why I had
JPOB   a lot of money in my apartment when the police came to my apartment
JPOB   at 6:00. I left Bobbie Ann in midtown Manhattan. She wanted to buy
JPOB   some clothes on Fifth Avenue.   I don't know where she is now.

Angel Rodriguez
Det., NYPD.

J. P. O'Brien. age 36
741 West Moor Lane, New Dorp, Staten Island.
O'Brien Used Cars, 257 Main Street, St. George, Staten Island.

An interrogation

Fill in the blanks with the correct tag questions.
You're John Patrick O'Brien, *aren't you?*

Police Detective: You're John Patrick O'Brien, • • • ?

O'Brien: Yes, I am.

PD: You're 36, • • • ?

O'B: Yes, that's right. It was my birthday yesterday.

PD: You sell used cars, • • • ?

O'B: Yes, I do. And other things.

PD: You live on Staten Island, • • • ?

O'B: Yes, I do. I live in New Dorp.

PD: You went to the races at Belmont yesterday, • • • ?

O'B: That's right.

PD: You weren't alone, • • • ?

O'B: No, I wasn't. I was with my— uh—friend, Bobbie Ann Chase.

PD: But you're married, • • • O'Brien?

O'B: Yes, but I haven't seen my wife for three years.

PD: I see. You left your apartment at eleven o'clock, • • • ?

O'B: Yes. About eleven.

PD: You were in your Corvette, • • • ?

O'B: Yes, I was.

PD: You didn't stop for gas, • • • ?

O'B: No.

PD: You had lunch at a Chinese restaurant, • • • ?

O'B: No, we didn't. We had lunch at a fast food place.

PD: You don't remember the name of the place, • • • ?

O'B: No, I'm afraid I don't.

PD: You had fried chicken, • • • ?

O'B: No, no. We got some hamburgers to go and ate in the car.

PD: You got to Belmont racetrack in time for the first race, • • • ?

O'B: Yes, correct.

PD: You were very lucky, • • • ?

O'B: Yes, I really was.

PD: You won $15,000, • • • ?

O'B: I can't remember exactly how much.

PD: There was $15,000 in your apartment, • • • ?

O'B: Really? You counted it; I didn't.

PD: You don't know where Bobbie Chase is now, • • • ?

O'B: No, I'm not her husband, • • • ?

PD: But you left her in midtown Manhattan because she wanted to buy some clothes.

O'B: Yes, that's right.

PD: It's interesting, • • • O'Brien? You've bought yourself a very, very fast car, • • • ?

O'B: What do you mean?

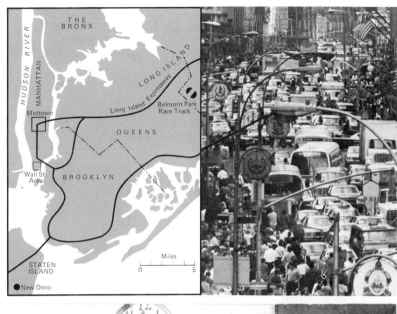

The last race at Belmont started late, and it didn't finish until twenty-five after five, so you drove from Belmont on Long Island to midtown Manhattan to Staten Island in 35 minutes—at rush hour! That's impossible, . . . , O'Brien!

29 Dinner with friends

Ken: Hello!
Peter: Hi, Ken. Hi, Donna. Come in. Let me take your coats.
Ken: Oh, thanks. What a nice house!
Peter: I'm glad you like it.
Ken: Where's Paula?
Peter: Oh, she's in the kitchen. She'll be here in a minute. Come into the living room. How about a drink before dinner?
Ken: That's a great idea! Do you have any bourbon?

kitchen/living room
bathroom/kitchen
bedroom/den
baby's room/living room

Paula: Here we are. Dinner's ready. Come to the table, everybody.
Donna: Thank you, Paula. Everything looks wonderful, and it smells delicious, too.
Paula: I'll put the salad in the middle of the table. Shall I serve you?
Donna: No, that's all right. We can help ourselves. Sit down and relax.
Paula: Peter, would you pour the wine, please? Ken, help yourself to vegetables, too.

salad/middle of the
  table/vegetables
vegetables/over here/
  salad
potatoes/at the end of
  the table/meat
meat/next to you/salad

Peter: Would you like some more brandy, Donna?
Donna: Oh, no, thanks. No more for me. I'm driving.
Peter: Oh, come on. Just a little bit.
Donna: No, really. I can't. I'll help Paula with the dishes.
Peter: No, no, don't worry. We always leave them till morning.

brandy
bourbon
wine
liqueur

Peter: Well, here are your coats.
Ken: Thanks. It's been a terrific evening. It was nice of you to invite us.
Peter: It was our pleasure. It was good to see you again.
Ken: We enjoyed ourselves a lot.
Peter: I'm glad. You have to come again soon.
Ken: Good night. And thanks again.
Peter: Good night. Drive carefully. It's a very wet night.

terrific/wet
wonderful/rainy
great/foggy
fabulous/icy

30 The bad boy of baseball

Reggie Walker, the Los Angeles Dodgers star, is in the news again. Yesterday he didn't show up for spring training. Last night, Willie Martin, the manager, was very upset. Reggie has had a lot of arguments with Martin. Martin spoke to our reporter, Warren Wolfe, last night.

WW: Where is Reggie, Willie?
WM: We don't know, Warren.
WW: When did you see him last?
WM: We spoke to each other five days ago. I haven't seen him since then.
WW: How upset are you?
WM: Very upset, Warren. This is the end. Reggie Walker won't play for us again.
WW: But Reggie's your best player, isn't he? Did he give a reason?
WM: No, he didn't.
WW: Does Reggie have any personal problems, Willie?
WM: I don't know, but he's a very selfish man. He only thinks about himself.

Warren Wolfe later spoke to Mrs. Louise Walker in the Walkers' one-million-dollar home in Beverly Hills.

WW: Where is Reggie, Louise?
LW: I don't know and I don't care.
WW: When did you see him last?
LW: We haven't seen each other for two weeks.
WW: Have you spoken to each other recently?
LW: No. We never want to see each other again.
WW: But why, Louise?
LW: Ask Reggie, Warren.

Our reporter, Warren Wolfe, found Reggie at his beach house in Acapulco. He was with Gina Alberghetti, the Italian actress. He seemed very happy.

WW: How long have you known each other, Reggie?
RW: We met each other at a disco three weeks ago. It was love at first sight.
WW: But what about your baseball career?
RW: Oh, baseball can wait. Gina is the most important thing in my life now. We love each other very much, and we understand each other.
WW: And your wife, Reggie? What about Louise?
RW: Oh, that ended a long time ago.
WW: What happened?
RW: Well, I was in love with Louise for a long time. We taught each other a lot, but . . . uh . . .
WW: But what?
RW: Well, we started to hate each other. We couldn't talk to each other. We couldn't even look at each other.
WW: So, Reggie, what are you going to do next?
RW: I don't know, Warren. Ask Gina!

Exercise

Look at this:
I haven't spoken to her. She hasn't spoken to me.
We haven't spoken to each other.

He met her. She met him.
They met each other.

Now you do the same:
1 I love her. She loves me.
2 He's seen her. She's seen him.
3 He needs her. She needs him.
4 I wrote to him. He wrote to me.
5 I've helped him. He's helped me.

31 So am I!

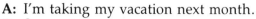

A: I'm taking my vacation next month.
B: So am I.
A: I need a change.
B: So do I. I'm tired of the same office and the same people every day!
A: Where are you going?
B: The Dominican Republic.
A: Really? I went there last year.
B: So did I. We always go to the Dominican Republic, but we never go to La Romana.
A: No, neither do I. There are too many Americans there. Where exactly are you going?
B: Sosua. It's a little town on the north coast.
A: You're joking!
B: No, I'm not. I've been there three times.
A: So have we. And we're going there this year too.
B: Not to the Hotel del Sol?
A: Yes, why?
B: Well, I'll see you there. That's my hotel too.

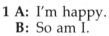

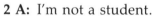

1 A: I'm happy.
  B: So am I.
  A: I'm not crazy.
  B: Neither am I.

2 A: I'm not a student.
  B: I am.
  A: I'm a teacher.
  B: I'm not.

3 A: I've read *War and Peace*.
  B: So have I.
  A: I haven't been to Haiti.
  B: Neither have I.

4 A: I haven't seen that movie.
  B: I have.
  A: I've studied a lot for the test.
  B: I haven't.

5 A: I like music.
  B: So do I.
  A: I don't like snakes.
  B: Neither do I.

6 A: I don't eat red meat.
  B: I do.
  A: I come to work on Sundays.
  B: I don't.

7 A: I was here last week.
  B: So was I.
  A: I wasn't late this morning.
  B: Neither was I.

8 A: I wasn't home yesterday.
  B: I was.
  A: I was bored last night.
  B: I wasn't.

9 A: I studied math in college.
  B: So did I.
  A: I didn't watch TV last night.
  B: Neither did I.

10 A: I didn't finish college.
   B: I did.
   A: I had wine with dinner last night.
   B: I didn't.

32 A family problem

826 Adams Street
Boston, Mass.

May 5

Dear Daddy,

Thank you very much for the birthday present. I was very pleased with the Porsche, but I didn't like the color, so I'm going to take it back and change it.

I saw Marc again yesterday. You're worried about him, aren't you? Well, don't worry about him. He's all right. He's very good at his job. He's a drummer in a rock group. I'm going to come home to New York next weekend. I'll bring Marc so you can meet him.

Love, Caroline

P.S. We love each other very much. He isn't interested in your money.

...as Berry Worthington III

May 15

Dear Caroline,

I'm sorry about last weekend. I was very upset with Marc, but he was very rude to me. I'm not a stupid old fool. I'm tired of dumb young men. I couldn't talk with him about anything. You love him, I know.

I just feel sorry for you, and I'm worried about your future. Marc likes rock music. He isn't interested in anything else. He isn't interested in you at all. You're making a terrible mistake. And I'm glad he isn't interested in my money because he isn't going to get any of it.

Love,
Dad

Exercise

I'm interested in politics.
What are you interested in?
I'm good at English, but I'm bad at math.
What about you?
I'm worried about money.
What about you?
I'm tired of this town.
What about you?
I'm very pleased with your English.
What about you?

33 The Yes/No Contest

Hi there! I'm Barry Smiles. Welcome to the "Yes/No Contest." Our rules are very simple. I'll ask you questions for 30 seconds. You must answer, but you can't answer with "Yes" or "No." You can't nod or shake your head either. Now, here is our first contestant, Anne Mock from Palm Beach, Florida.

Smiles: What's your name?
Anne: Anne. Anne Mock.
Smiles: Where are you from, Anne?
Anne: Palm Beach.
Smiles: Did you say Palm Springs?
Anne: No, Palm . . . (*Gong!*)
Smiles: Oh, I'm sorry, Anne. You said "No." Our next contestant is Chuck Fleener from St.Louis, Missouri. It's *Doctor* Fleener, isn't it?
Chuck: That's right, but call me Chuck.
Smiles: Fine. You aren't nervous, are you, Chuck?
Chuck: I'm not nervous.
Smiles: Did you shake your head?
Chuck: I didn't.
Smiles: Are you sure?
Chuck: Yes, I'm . . . (*Gong!*)
Smiles: Oh! I'm sorry, Chuck. Better luck next time. Now, here's our third contestant. He's Richard Oropallo from Washington, D.C. Hello, Richard.
Richard: Hello, Barry.
Smiles: You work in a bank, don't you?
Richard: That's correct.
Smiles: Do you like your job?
Richard: I enjoy it very much.
Smiles: Oh, do you?
Richard: I said, "I enjoy it very much."
Smiles: Now, you aren't married, are you?
Richard: I am married.
Smiles: Is your wife here tonight?
Richard: She's at home in Washington.
Smiles: So she isn't here.
Richard: Of course not.
Smiles: Do you have any children?
Richard: I have two children.
Smiles: Two boys?
Richard: A boy and a girl.
Smiles: And . . . (*Buzz!*) That's 30 seconds! You've done it, Richard! Isn't that wonderful, everybody? He's won tonight's jackpot prize—a brand new, fully automatic dishwasher!

Look at these expressions

Yes	*No*	
That's right.	That's wrong.	I don't know.
That's correct.	That isn't correct.	I'm not sure.
Of course.	Of course not.	
That's true.	That isn't true.	I'm not certain.
I agree.	I disagree.	

34 I used to . . .

A: Hello, Tom? This is your Dad—your old Dad in the nursing home. Why aren't you here?

B: Oh, hi, Dad. Uh—I'm very busy. I can't visit you today. Uh—I'm sorry, Dad.

A: Tom, Tom! You used to visit me. You used to take me to the movies. You used to bring Barbara and the children.

B: I'm sorry, Dad. We'll come for your birthday.

A: My birthday! It's today! At least you used to call. You didn't even send a card. I'm writing a new will!

C: Hello, Dolores.

D: Oh, hi, Tony. How are you?

C: Well, uh—not very well.

D: Really? What's wrong?

C: I feel so tired all the time.

D: But, Tony, you used to have so much energy.

C: I know. When I was young, I used to work twelve hours a day.

D: Tony, you're only 28 years old!

C: I know, I know.

D: Well, stop complaining. Take some vitamins.

C: I've heard all this before!

D: No, really, Tony. Take Nature Plus vitamin pills. They work.

C: O.K. I'll try them.

E: Reggie, you used to be the best baseball player in the National League. Are you going to come back and play again?

F: No, I'm not. No way.

E: Why not?

F: Well, baseball used to be the most important thing in my life, but it isn't anymore. I used to practice every day. I never used to smoke, drink, or stay up late.

E: Why has your life changed, Reggie?

F: Well, I was poor then, but I'm not now. I don't need to play baseball any more!

G: Dad?

H: What?

G: There's a terrific movie downtown.

H: Really? What is it?

G: *War in Space.*

H: Are you going to see it?

G: I'd like to. All of my friends are going, but I don't have any money.

H: O.K. O.K. How much do you want?

G: Ten dollars.

H: Ten dollars! When I was your age I used to get two dollars to go to the movies!

G: I know, I know. And you used to walk a mile to school, and you used to cut wood—

H: And I used to talk to my father with respect!

Exercise

I used to eat a lot of candy when I was young, but I don't any more.
What about you?
What did you use to do when you were young, that you don't do any more?

Write four sentences.

35 A busy office

Jay Power: Yes, Janice, what is it?

Janice Mills: Bob Hudson wants to speak to you.

Jay Power: I'm very busy right now. Ask him to call back later.

Janice Mills: All right.

Jay Power: Oh, and Janice, tell Chris to photocopy the president's report.

Janice Mills: O.K. Anything else?

Jay Power: Yes. Tell Helen not to call her boyfriend on the office phone.

Janice Mills: All right, I will.

Janice Mills: Hello? This is Mr. Power's secretary again.

Bob Hudson: Yes?

Janice Mills: I'm afraid Mr. Power's very busy right now. Can you call back later?

Bob Hudson: All right. What about this afternoon?

Janice Mills: Yes, that'll be fine.

Janice Mills: Oh, Chris?

Chris Day: Yes, Janice?

Janice Mills: Mr. Power wants you to photocopy this report.

Chris Day: O.K. I'll do it later.

Janice Mills: No, Chris. Do it now. I know it's important.

Janice Mills: Helen, did you call your boyfriend on the office phone yesterday?

Helen Biagi: Well—uh—yes. I did. But it was urgent.

Janice Mills: Hmm. I think Mr. Power heard you. He wasn't very pleased about it. Don't use the office phone for personal calls.

Helen Biagi: Yes. O.K., Janice. I won't do it again. I'm sorry.

Jay Power: Janice, did you speak to Bob Hudson?

Janice Mills: Yes, I did. I asked him to call back later. He says he'll call you this afternoon.

Jay Power: Fine. Has Chris photocopied that report yet?

Janice Mills: Not yet, but I told him to do it immediately. I think he's doing it now.

Jay Power: Good. Did you tell Helen not to call her boyfriend from here.

Janice Mills: Yes, I told her not to use the office phone for personal calls. She says she won't do it again. I'm sure she won't.

Jay Power: Well, I hope she won't. Her boyfriend is living in Saudi Arabia!

Look at this

"Ask him to call back later."
"Can you call back later?"
She asked him to call back later.

"Tell her not to use the telephone."
"Please don't use the telephone."
She told her not to use the telephone.

Exercise

"I can't do it." (he says)
He says he can't do it.

1 "That'll be all right." (she thinks)
2 "It's important." (she knows)
3 "I'm busy." (he's afraid)
4 "She won't do it again." (she's sure)
5 "She called her boyfriend." (she's sorry)
6 "Her boyfriend is living in Saudia Arabia." (he says)

36 The smuggler

Latka was a customs officer in Europe. He used to work in a small border town. It wasn't a busy town, and there wasn't much work. The road was usually very quiet, and there weren't many travelers. It wasn't a very interesting job, but Latka liked an easy life. About once a week, he used to meet an old man. His name was Spevna. He always used to arrive at the border early in the morning in a big truck. The truck was always empty. After a while Latka became suspicious. He often used to search the truck, but he never found anything. One day he asked Spevna about his job. Spevna laughed and said, ''I'm a smuggler.''

Last year Latka immigrated to the United States. One night he was having dinner in a restaurant in Los Angeles. On the other side of the restaurant he saw Spevna drinking champagne. Latka walked over to him.

Latka: Hello, there!
Spevna: Hi!
Latka: Do you remember me?
Spevna: Yes, of course I do. You're a customs officer.
Latka: I used to be, but I'm not any more. I retired last year, and I live in Los Angeles now. I often used to search your truck.
Spevna: But you never found anything!
Latka: No, I didn't. Can I ask you something?
Spevna: Of course you can.
Latka: Were you a smuggler?
Spevna: Of course I was.
Latka: But the truck was always empty. What were you smuggling?
Spevna: Trucks!

37 I'm bored

Jim: I'm bored!
Jean: Well, do something interesting.
Jim: What, for instance?
Jean: Go to the movies.
Jim: Movies bore me.
Jean: All of them?
Jim: Movies today are so boring. I'm not interested in sex and violence.
Jean: Well, what interests you then?
Jim: Nothing!
Jean: You need some fresh air and exercise.

Helen: Have you heard the news, Bill?
Bill: No, why?
Helen: A war has just started in Mandanga.
Bill: Mandanga? Where's that?
Helen: I don't know exactly, but it's disturbing. They showed a report on TV this morning.
Bill: Well, I'm not disturbed. I never watch the news these days. I like sports programs.
Helen: Why aren't you interested in the news?
Bill: Well, all the news is bad. I work hard all day, and I just want entertainment in the evening.

Wendy: What are you doing tonight, Michelle?
Michelle: I'm staying home. There's a good horror movie on TV.
Wendy: What is it?
Michelle: *The Blood of Frankenstein.*
Wendy: Oh, I've seen it. It's really frightening.
Michelle: Frightening? I think horror movies are amusing.
Wendy: Amusing? Horror movies?
Michelle: Yes. I went with Anne to see *Dracula II* last week. I was very amused. I laughed from beginning to end.
Wendy: What about Anne?
Michelle: Oh, she was terrified. She was under the seat.

Nick: Did you go to the football game last Saturday?
Ben: I watched it on TV.
Nick: It was very exciting, wasn't it?
Ben: My brother went, and he was so excited near the end that he threw his hat in the air when Hershell ran that touchdown.
Nick: Did he find his hat?
Ben: Yes, but it was a little embarrassing. He had to ask a cop for it.

Look at this

I'm bored.	It's boring.	It bores me.
She's interested.	It's interesting.	It interests her.
She's disturbed.	It's disturbing.	It disturbs her.
We're frightened.	It's frightening.	It frightens us.
You're amused.	It's amusing.	It amuses you.
They're terrified.	It's terrifying.	It terrifies them.
I'm excited.	It's exciting.	It excites me.
He's embarrassed.	It's embarrassing.	It embarrasses him.

38 Advice

Phyllis: What's the matter, Annie? You look worried.
Annie: I am. I'm getting very fat.
Phyllis: Oh, but you're not.
Annie: Oh, but I am. I just bought some new jeans, and I can't get them on. They're too tight. I have to lose weight.
Phyllis: Well, maybe you should go on a diet.
Annie: I know, but what kind of diet?
Phyllis: You should eat lots of salad and fruit.
Annie: But I don't like salad. I prefer meat.
Phyllis: Well, you can eat meat, but you shouldn't eat much. You shouldn't eat bread or potatoes either.
Annie: What about alcohol? Can I drink wine?
Phyllis: Oh, no! You should never drink alcohol on a diet.

Miguel: What's the matter, Dario? You don't look happy.
Dario: I'm not. I'm worried about my English.
Miguel: What's the problem?
Dario: I'm not practicing enough.
Miguel: Why not?
Dario: Well, it's hard to meet Americans.
Miguel: You should go out more.
Dario: Where should I go?
Miguel: Maybe you should join a club or an exercise class.
Dario: But Americans never speak to me.
Miguel: Well, you should speak first.
Dario: What can I talk about?
Miguel: The weather! Americans are always interested in the weather!

Karen: Hello, Stanley. You look tired today.
Stanley: Yes, I'm working too hard.
Karen: You should take a few days off.
Stanley: I know I should, but we're just too busy. I'm working twelve hours a day.
Karen: Twelve hours a day! You're going to kill yourself!
Stanley: What else can I do?
Karen: Maybe you should quit.
Stanley: I can't. I need the money.

Exercise

Write sentences with *should* and *shouldn't*:
1 Your friend wants to lose weight.
2 Someone wants to learn your language.
3 Your friend wants to be a millionaire—right away.

39 An evening out

Steve: Do you want to eat out tonight?
Carol: Which restaurant would you like to go to?
Steve: How about the Flamenco?
Carol: The Flamenco? Which one is that?
Steve: Don't you remember? That's the one that serves seafood.
Carol: Oh, yes! Sure, let's go there.

Carol: Look over there.
Steve: Where?
Carol: In the corner. It's Ray Powell, isn't it?
Steve: Where? I don't see him.
Carol: There. He's the one that's wearing a tuxedo.
Steve: Oh. The one that's talking so loudly. What about him?
Carol: Don't you remember? He went to college with us. He was the only one that didn't finish his degree.
Steve: Hmm. Oh, yes. Well, he looks successful. What does he do now?
Carol: Nothing. He doesn't have to work.
Steve: Why not?
Carol: You remember, don't you? He married Patty Hetty.
Steve: Patty Hetty?
Carol: Yes, the girl that inherited a fortune. Her father was a millionaire.
Steve: Oh, yes, right. Isn't she the one that died in a plane crash?
Carol: That's right, and he got all the money.

That's the one that did it!

Look at this:

A boy broke the window.

Is that the boy?
Yes, that's the boy that broke the window.

Some letters arrived this morning.

Are these the letters?
Yes, those are the letters that arrived this morning.

Now you do the same.

A man met the President.

Is that the man?

They won the medals.

Are those the men?

A car crashed.

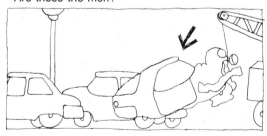

Is that the car?

A dog attacked the mail carrier.

Is that the dog?

40 I've been waiting . . .

Chris: Hi, Janice. Is the boss in?
Janice: Yes, he is, Chris. He's in his office, and he's waiting for you.
Chris: Oh. What time did he get in?
Janice: He got in at twenty to ten.
Chris: Twenty to ten! So he's been waiting for twenty minutes. Wow! I'm in trouble.

Diane: Hello, Judy. You've been sitting here for an hour. Where's Stephen?
Judy: Hi, Diane. He's dancing with Peggy.
Diane: Oh, yes. I see him. Has he been dancing all evening?
Judy: Yes, he has. But he hasn't been dancing with me.

Alice Perry: Well, Vera Parker. Hello! Are you waiting to see Doctor Lightfoot?
Vera Parker: Hi, Alice. Yes, I am.
Alice Perry: How long have you been waiting?
Vera Parker: Well, let's see. I've been waiting since nine o'clock.
Alice Perry: So you haven't been waiting long. It's only ten after nine.
Vera Parker: Right, I haven't. I've been reading this magazine. There's an interesting article about operations.

Sally: Eric, call the waiter again!
Eric: I've been trying to call him, Sally.
Sally: But, Eric, we've been sitting here for twenty minutes, and I'm not going to wait any longer.
Eric: I'm sorry, Sally, but he's talking to that woman.
Sally: Yes, I see. He's been talking to her since we came in.
Eric: Waiter!
Waiter: Yes, sir. Do you want your check?
Sally: The check! We haven't even seen the menu yet!

Exercise

He's waiting. He arrived five minutes ago.
He's been waiting for five minutes.

They're waiting. They arrived at nine o'clock.
They've been waiting since nine o'clock.

Continue
1 She's sitting in the chair. She sat down ten minutes ago.
2 They're watching television. They turned it on at eight o'clock.
3 He's writing a letter. He started fifteen minutes ago.
4 She's listening to the radio. She turned it on at seven-thirty.
5 They're talking to each other. They met five minutes ago.

41 A court case

A few months ago, there was a bank robbery in San Francisco. The police arrested a man and a woman. They're in court now. Jessica Yamaguchi saw the robbery. She's on the witness stand. The judge and the twelve members of the jury are listening to her. A lawyer is asking her some questions.

Lawyer: Now, Mrs. Yamaguchi. You saw the bank robbery, didn't you?
Mrs. Yamaguchi: Yes, I did.
Lawyer: You saw a man, didn't you?
Mrs. Yamaguchi: That's right. I saw him when he went into the bank and when he came out.
Lawyer: Now, look around the court. Do you see that man?
Mrs. Yamaguchi: Yes. He's the one! He's the man I saw.
Lawyer: He wasn't alone when he went into the bank, was he?
Mrs. Yamaguchi: No, he wasn't. He was with a woman.
Lawyer: Now, do you see that woman in the court?
Mrs. Yamaguchi: Yes. There! She's the woman I saw.
Lawyer: I see, Mrs. Yamaguchi. Now look at the man and woman again. This is very important. Are you absolutely sure about them?
Mrs. Yamaguchi: Absolutely sure. They're the people I saw.
Lawyer: Now, Mrs. Yamaguchi, what was the man wearing when he went into the bank?

Mrs. Yamaguchi: I don't remember everything, but I remember his hat and his bag.
Lawyer: Look at Exhibit A on the table. Is that the hat?
Mrs. Yamaguchi: Yes, that's the hat he was wearing.
Lawyer: And Exhibit B?
Mrs. Yamaguchi: Yes, that's the bag he was carrying.
Lawyer: Do you remember anything about the woman?
Mrs. Yamaguchi: Yes. She was wearing a black wig and red platform shoes.
Lawyer: How do you know she was wearing a wig, Mrs. Yamaguchi?
Mrs. Yamaguchi: Because it fell off when she was running to the car.
Lawyer: Look at Exhibit C on the table. Is that the wig?
Mrs. Yamaguchi: Yes, that's the wig she was wearing.
Lawyer: And Exhibit D. Look at the shoes.
Mrs. Yamaguchi: Yes, they're the shoes she was wearing.
Lawyer: Thank you, Mrs. Yamaguchi.

Exercise

They're the people.
She saw them.
They're the people she saw.

1 She's the girl.
  He kissed her.
2 Those are the shoes.
  He was wearing them.
3 That's the house.
  He's going to buy it.
4 That's the book.
  She's been reading it.

42 The Empty Chair

A friend of mine in Boston, Jerry Streisen, almost had a nervous breakdown last year. I told him to go to a doctor.

Doctor: Hello, Mr. Streisen. What's the problem?
Jerry: Well, doctor, I'm very tense and nervous. I haven't been able to sleep for several days.
Doctor: Hmm. Have you been working hard?
Jerry: Yes, I've been working twelve hours a day.
Doctor: Have you been taking any pills?
Jerry: No, but I have been smoking too much, and I've been drinking a lot of coffee.
Doctor: Well, you should take a few days off. You should go someplace quiet and peaceful, like Nantucket.

Jerry decided to go to Nantucket the next weekend. He had to take a boat from New Bedford to Nantucket and arrived late Friday evening. He rang the doorbell of a boardinghouse, and Mrs. Searcy, the owner, answered the door. Then she showed him to his room. Jerry was very tired and went straight to bed. He slept well and didn't wake up until nine o'clock the next morning.

Jerry went downstairs for breakfast. Because there weren't any other guests, Mrs. Searcy invited him to have breakfast with her and her daughter, Catherine. Catherine was already sitting in the dining room. She was about thirteen years old, with long black hair and clear gray eyes. Mrs. Searcy went to the kitchen to make breakfast. Jerry and Catherine looked at each other nervously for a few seconds.

Jerry: There are four places at the table. Is there another guest?
Catherine: No. We never talk about the empty place.
Jerry: "The empty place?" What do you mean?
Catherine: Well, that used to be my father's place.
Jerry: "Used to be?" I don't understand.
Catherine: My father liked to go fishing. Three years ago he went out on his boat, and he never came back.
Jerry: What happened to him?
Catherine: Nobody knows. They searched everywhere, but they never found anything. My mother always keeps that place for him, and she makes his breakfast every morning. She thinks he'll come back. That's a picture of him . . . over there on the wall. My mother's been waiting for him for three years.

Jerry said nothing, but he looked very worried. At that moment, Mrs. Searcy came into the room. She poured four cups of coffee and put one cup at the empty place. Jerry looked more worried, and he stared at the empty chair. Suddenly, he heard footsteps outside the door, and a tall man with a black beard walked into the room. Jerry looked terrified. It was the man in the picture! Jerry jumped up and ran out of the room.

Man: Who was that? What's the matter with him?
Mrs. Searcy: I don't know. I don't understand. He's a guest from Boston. He arrived last night after you went to sleep.
Man: Catherine, do you know anything about this?
Catherine: No, Daddy, I don't. But he's here because he's very nervous. He says he's hiding here because a tall man with a black beard is trying to kill him.
Man: Catherine, have you been telling stories again?
Catherine (*laughing*): Stories, Daddy? Me?

43 How long? How much?

Bank Officer: Please have a seat.
Esther Rosales: Thank you. I'm Esther Rosales. I've had an account here for ten years.
Bank Officer: What can I do for you, Mrs. Rosales?
Esther Rosales: Well, I want to borrow some money.
Bank Officer: What for?
Esther Rosales: I want to buy a car. I've been saving for two years.
Bank Officer: How much have you saved?
Esther Rosales: I've saved about two thousand dollars.

Pablo: What are you reading?
Wayne: *The Godfather*. It's about the Mafia. I've never seen the movie, and Bruce told me to read it.
Pablo: It's a very long book.
Wayne: I know. I've been reading it for a month, and I haven't finished it yet!
Pablo: How many pages have you read?
Wayne: About 400. I don't like long books.
Pablo: Neither do I.

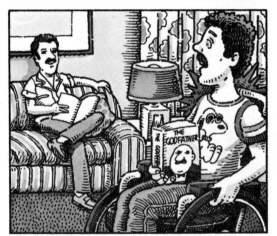

Attendant: Yes, ma'am. What can I do for you?
Driver: Hi! Fill it up, please.
Attendant: Regular or unleaded?
Driver: Unleaded. It's nearly empty. I've been driving all day.
Attendant: Oh? How far have you driven?
Driver: About 400 miles . . . from Atlanta.
Attendant: That's a long way. Check the oil?
Driver: Yes, O.K.

Brenda: Hi, Helen. Are you still working? It's time for lunch.
Helen: I know. But I haven't finished these letters yet. They're important. Mr. Power wants them this afternoon.
Brenda: How long have you been typing?
Helen: Since nine o'clock. I haven't even stopped for coffee.
Brenda: How many have you done?
Helen: Most of them. There are only two left.
Brenda: Well, do them after lunch.
Helen: No, I want to finish them now.
Brenda: O.K. See you later.

Exercise 1

She/two years/$2000.
She's been saving for two years.
She's saved $2000.

Now you do the same:
They/six months/$1600.
He/a year/$3000.
We/three years/$6000.

Exercise 2

I/*The Godfather*/a month/ 400 pages.
I've been reading The Godfather, *for a month.*
I've read 400 pages.

Now you do the same:
He/*War and Peace*/a week/250 pages.
She/*Moby Dick*/two weeks/300 pages.
I/*Gone With the Wind*/ten days/500 pages.

Exercise 3

They/all day/400 miles/ Atlanta.
They've been driving all day.
They've driven 400 miles.
They've driven from Atlanta.

Now you do the same:
He/since nine o'clock/300 miles/Dallas.
We/for six hours/250 miles/Tampa.
She/since breakfast/350 miles/Memphis.

Exercise 4

I/letters/typing/nine o'clock.
I haven't finished these letters.
I've been typing since nine o'clock.

Now you do the same:
She/report/writing/ yesterday afternoon.
He/article/reading/ten o'clock.
We/housework/cleaning/ breakfast.

44 Look!

Nick Kaneohe is a guide for Mauna Loa Tours. Some new tourists have just arrived in Honolulu from Japan. He's showing them around the Waikiki section. "I'm sure you'll enjoy your stay here. There's the beach that's the safest for surfers. And that's the restaurant that sells picnic lunches. Over there's the store that sells the best souvenirs. I'll meet you back here at four o'clock. We'll take buses to the luau. Have fun!"

Anne used to live in Cartagena, Colombia. She is showing Lee some pictures she took there. "Look. This is the house I rented. And here's the restaurant I used to go to. I used to eat there every Saturday. And this is the school I used to teach at. And this is the beach I used to lie on. It was a wonderful place."

Mike's just had an accident. He's telling a police officer about it. "The car in front of me stopped suddenly. I managed to stop, but the van behind me didn't. It hit my car and pushed it into the car in front of me. There's my car. There's the van that hit my car. And that's the car my car hit."

Anne is showing Lee an old school picture. "That's Miss Kate Clark in the middle. She's the one that taught us Latin. Her classes were very boring. The fat man on the left is Mr. Dillard. He's the one that used to give us nightmares. Señor Pardo's on the right. He's the one that taught us Spanish . . . and art. I was never bored in his classes!"

This is a picture of Frank Corman. He's the man the police arrested yesterday. He's standing next to Elizabeth Martin. Martin's the police officer that caught him.

Exercise

Look at these examples:
She's the girl. I love her.
She's the girl I love.

He's the man. He met me.
He's the man that met me.

That's the plane. I flew in it.
That's the plane I flew in.

It's the gun. It killed him.
It's the gun that killed him.

Now you do the same.
He's the man. He visited Buenos Aires.
She's the girl. I know her.
They're the shoes. I was wearing them.
That's the man. He lives near me.
There's the bridge. We crossed it.
There's the house. We used to live in it.
Those are the packages. They arrived this morning.
That's the woman. She'll be president of the company some day.
He's the man. I spoke to him.
It's the car. It crashed.

45 Another letter from Mary

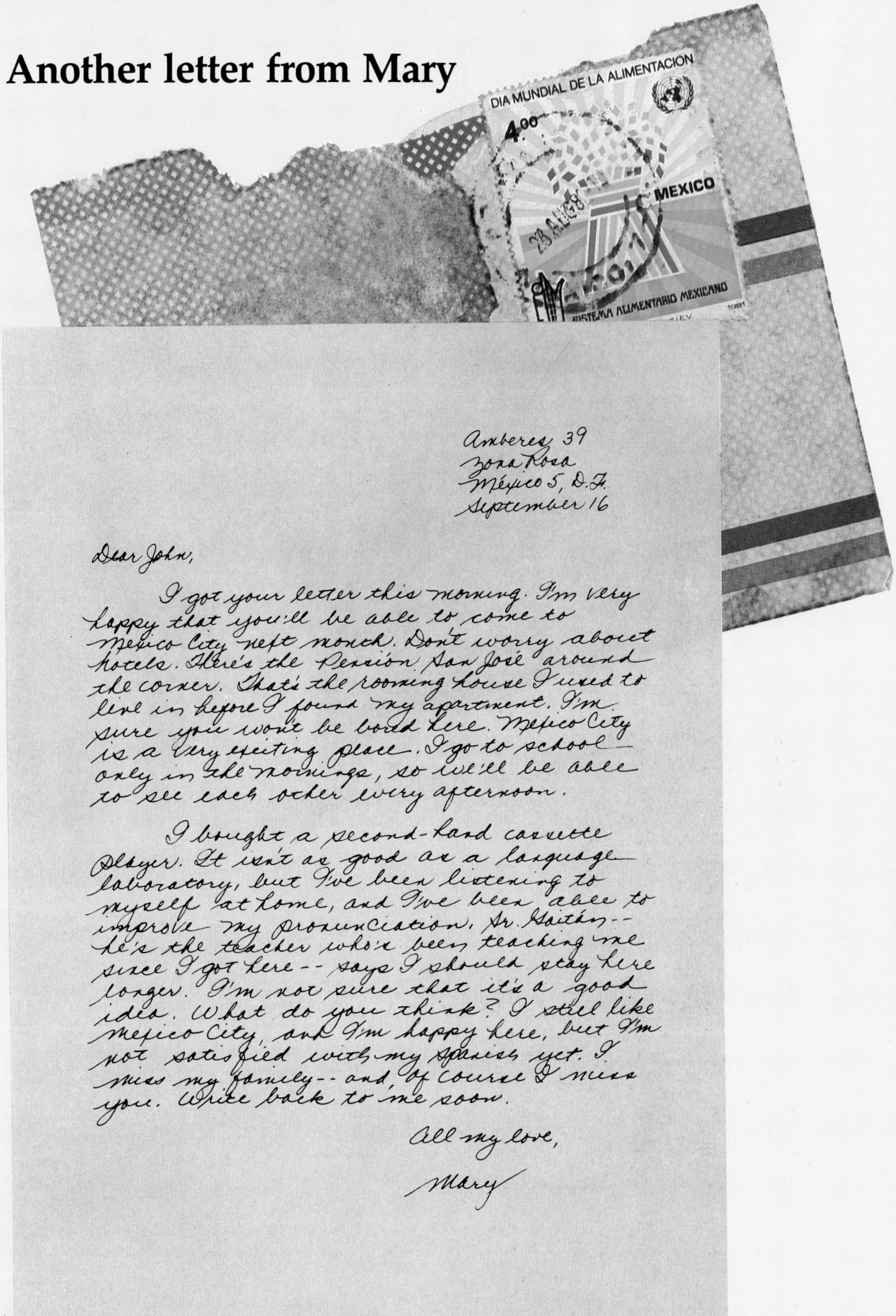

[Handwritten letter:]

Amberes 39
Zona Rosa
México 5, D.F.
September 16

Dear John,

I got your letter this morning. I'm very happy that you'll be able to come to Mexico City next month. Don't worry about hotels. There's the Pensión San José around the corner. That's the rooming house I used to live in before I found my apartment. I'm sure you won't be bored here. Mexico City is a very exciting place. I go to school only in the mornings, so we'll be able to see each other every afternoon.

I bought a second-hand cassette player. It isn't as good as a language laboratory, but I've been listening to myself at home, and I've been able to improve my pronunciation. Mr. Gaither — he's the teacher who's been teaching me since I got here — says I should stay here longer. I'm not sure that it's a good idea. What do you think? I still like Mexico City, and I'm happy here, but I'm not satisfied with my Spanish yet. I miss my family — and, of course I miss you. Write back to me soon.

All my love,

Mary

Look at this example

I/postcard/afternoon.
I/happy/you/able/here/week.
I got your postcard this afternoon. I'm happy that you'll be able to come here next week.

Now use these words and write a letter.

I/postcard/afternoon.
I/happy/you/able/here/week.
Don't worry/a place to stay.
There/a Holiday Inn/block.
That/hotel/I/stay/before/new roommate.
I/sure/you won't/bored.
This/interesting town.
I/class/afternoons/so/we/meet/evening.
I/new tape recorder.

Tape recorder/portable cassette player.
I/myself/home, and I/improve/accent.
Ms. Smith . . . she/teacher/me/came here . . . says I/longer.
I think/good idea.
What/think?
I/this town and/happy/but I/not satisfied/English yet.
I/everybody.
Write/soon.

46 Planning ahead

A: Hello? Samba Restaurant.
B: I'd like to make a reservation for tonight.
A: All right. What time?
B: Eight o'clock.
A: Eight o'clock. For how many?
B: There are ten of us.
A: Ten! We don't usually take large parties.
B: I know, but we are regular customers.
A: What's your name, please?
B: Diana Ross.
A: Miss Ross! Of course, that'll be all right. Party of ten at eight.

tonight/8 o'clock/ten
tomorrow night/9:30/ eight
Saturday evening/8:45/ seven
next Friday/ten o'clock/ nine

C: I'd like to get two seats for the concert on Thursday.
D: Where would you like to sit?
C: I'm not sure.
D: Well, here's a seating plan of the concert hall.
C: How much is it in the middle section?
D: $15.
C: $15! That's a little too expensive for us. How much is it here in the back?
D: $9.
C: That's fine. What time does the concert start?
D: At 8:00.

concert/Thursday/8:00

rock concert/Friday night/10:00

ballet/Saturday afternoon/3:00

opera/Monday evening / 7:30

in the middle section—$15
in the front—$20
on the left side—$12
on the right side—$12

E: Do you have any seats left on the Bay Area tour tomorrow?
F: Yes, we do. There are a few seats left.
E: Is that the tour that includes the Sonoma Valley?
F: That's right.
E: How long does the whole tour take?
F: About seven hours.
E: Should I pay you now?
F: If you don't mind.

San Francisco Tours
Bay Area and Sonoma Valley (7 hours)
Sausalito and Muir Woods (6 hours)
Sonoma and Napa Wineries (8 hours)
San Francisco and Berkeley (4 hours)
Golden Gate Bridge and Marin County (5 hours)

G: Good morning. Mohawk Hair Stylists.
H: Hello. I'd like to make an appointment for three o'clock this afternoon—with Monique.
G: Let's see. I'm afraid Monique's busy at three.
H: Oh, no! Monique always cuts my hair.
G: I'm sorry.
H: Well, how about four o'clock?
G: I'm really sorry, but Monique's busy all afternoon.
H: Oh, no! What a mess!
G: What can I say? I'm really very sorry, but you should always call a few days in advance.

3:00/Monique
2:40/Paolo
12:30/Kenneth
5:00/Teresa

47 A new job

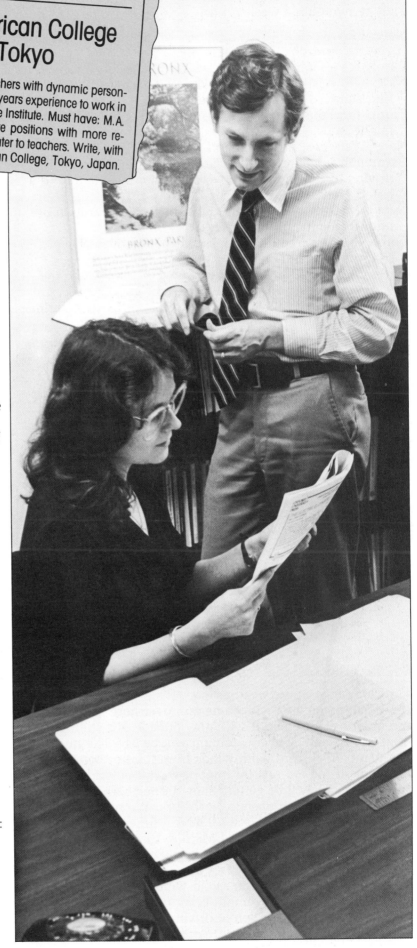

Maureen: Jeff, have you seen this ad in the *ESL Newsletter*?

Jeff: Yes, I saw it, but I'm not interested in finding a new job. I've been here since I finished my Ph.D. I like working here.

Maureen: Really? I've only been here for two years, and I'm already tired of doing the same thing every day. I'm afraid of getting really bored.

Jeff: Oh, come on! It's not that bad. You'll do the same thing there every day.

Maureen: But the salaries are good.

Jeff: I'm not interested in making more money. I have enough now.

Maureen: I can never have enough. Of course you live at home with your parents.

Jeff: I like living with my parents. What's wrong with that?

Maureen: Nothing. But I like being independent. I like traveling. I enjoy meeting new people. I'm going to apply for the job.

Jeff: Well, good luck.

Exercise 1

Answer these questions:

What do you like doing | on weekends?
                          | on vacations?

What do you enjoy doing in the | spring?
                                   | summer?
                                   | fall?
                                   | winter?

Exercise 2

I don't like watching TV.
Write five true sentences.

Exercise 3

flying
He's afraid of flying.

Write sentences using:
going to the dentist
losing his job
dying

Exercise 4

I'm interested in learning English.
I'm not interested in studying history.
Write true sentences.

48 The weather forecast

Carol and Nathan Ackerman live in Washington, D.C.
They're planning a weekend trip.

Nate: I know, Carol! Why don't we go to the Pennsylvania
Dutch country?
Carol: It's a long way, Nate.
Nate: Oh, it isn't too far. Anyway, the highway's an
Interstate, so we can get there quickly.
Carol: But Pennsylvania's often cold at this time of year. It
might snow.
Nate: Well, yes. It might, but I don't think it will.
Carol: I'm not sure. It is December, and I'm afraid of
driving in the snow. And we might not be able to find a
hotel. They might be closed.
Nate: Oh, that's no problem. I can make a reservation by
phone tonight.
Carol: Well, maybe it's not a bad idea. We might have
beautiful weather.
Nate: Oh, we'll enjoy ourselves anyway. Let's watch the
weather forecast on TV. We might not go to
Pennsylvania. We might go to Virginia or North Carolina.
We can decide after the forecast.

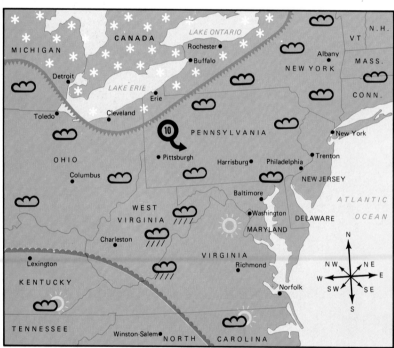

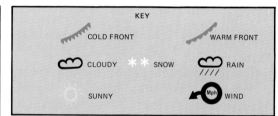

TODAY		TOMORROW	
HIGH	51°	HIGH	36°
LOW	34°	LOW	28°
NOW	43°	RAIN	
Humidity 55%		OR SNOW	
CLEAR			

Let's look now at the weather map. It's generally clear in
the Washington area with some rain over here in the
mountains of Virginia. It's 43° now outside our studio.
That's 6° Celsius. Our low tonight will be 34°. The humidity
is a damp 75 percent, with winds from the northwest. Now
let's look at the forecast for tomorrow. It'll be colder, with a
high of 36°. They'll be getting snow in northern
Pennsylvania and in upstate New York. We might get some
of the snow, but probably we'll have a little rain instead.
The rest of the Northeast and Middle Atlantic states will be
gray and overcast, except it'll be partly cloudy with
occasional sunshine south of us in Virginia and North
Carolina. We might get some cold winds tomorrow from
the northwest, and they might bring us some of that snow.
So keep that in mind if you're driving this weekend,
because Sunday looks like more of the same.

Exercise 1

*Where's Philadelphia? It's in eastern
Pennsylvania.*

Write questions and answers for:
Pittsburgh, Richmond, New York, Trenton,
Cleveland, Detroit, Buffalo, Norfolk,
Baltimore, Charleston.

Exercise 2

*What will the weather be like in Pittsburgh
tomorrow? It will snow.*
*What will the weather be like in Baltimore?
It might snow or rain.*

Write questions and answers for all the cities.

Exercise 3

What will the weather be like here tomorrow?

49 A restaurant kitchen

Waitress: Hurry up, Chef! I have 12 customers, and they all want today's special. Some of them have been waiting for 15 minutes. They're getting upset.

Chef: I know, I know, but I only have two hands. You'll have to help me.

Waitress: Help you? That's not my job. I'm a waitress, not a cook.

Chef: Well, one of my assistants is off today, and the other is out sick.

Waitress: Oh, O.K. What do I do first?

Chef: Well, start putting the meat on the plates, and I'll finish these vegetables.

Waitress: O.K. Is that enough meat?

Chef: Hmm. That's a little too much. Take some off.

Waitress: What about potatoes?

Chef: Oh, put on plenty of potatoes— they're cheap—and lots of peas.

Waitress: All right. Can I take them out now?

Chef: Have you put the gravy on yet?

Waitress: Huh? Oh, no, I haven't. Where is it?

Chef: Here it is.

Waitress: Oh, there isn't enough gravy.

Chef: There's plenty in that pot over there.

Waitress: Here? O.K. I've got it.

Chef: Fine. Now you can begin taking the plates out to the customers.

Waitress: Whew! They're hot!

Chef: Well, use a dish towel. And don't carry too many plates. You might drop them.

Waitress: Oh, I won't drop them. I've never dropped a plate in my life!
(*Crash!*)

Exercise

Thirty-two people have bought tickets for a city tour.
This is a forty-seat bus.
There are plenty of seats.
This is a thirty-seat bus.
There aren't enough seats.

1
Eight people are coming to dinner.
We have twelve wine glasses.
We only have seven chairs.

2
This car costs $10,000. Both Helen and Barry want to buy it.
Helen has $12,000.
Barry only has $9,000.

50 Asking for directions

A: Excuse me.
B: Yes? Can I help you?
A: I'm looking for the men's shoe department.
B: It's on the third floor. The escalator is over there.
A: Thank you.

BLOOMBERGER'S
6th floor
Cafeteria, records, books
5th floor
Furniture
4th floor
China, crystal, linens
3rd floor
Men's clothing
2nd floor
Ladies' clothing
1st floor
Cosmetics, accessories
Basement
Food boutique, kitchenware

C: Good morning. Can I help you?
D: Yes. I have an appointment with Mrs. Bedoya, the sales manager.
C: What time is your appointment?
D: Eleven-thirty.
C: Right. You're Ms. O'Hare, aren't you?
D: Yes, that's right.
C: Take the elevator to the third floor. Go down the hall to the left. Mrs. Bedoya's office is the third door on the right. You can't miss it.
D: Thank you.
C: Don't bother to knock. Just go right in. She's expecting you.

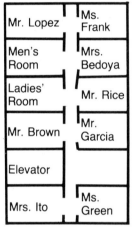

Mr. Lopez	Ms. Frank
Men's Room	Mrs. Bedoya
Ladies' Room	Mr. Rice
Mr. Brown	Mr. Garcia
Elevator	
Mrs. Ito	Ms. Green

E: Excuse me.
F: Yes?
E: I'm lost. Is this the way to Wakulla?
F: No, you're on the wrong road. This is US 19 going south to Tampa.
E: Oh, no. Well, can you tell me the way to Wakulla?
F: Go back about 20 miles and turn left on 319, then go about 4 miles and left again on 363.
E: 319 then 363?
F: That's right. 363 is the road to Wakulla. You'll see signs along the way.

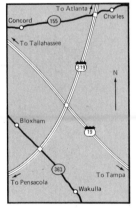

G: Does this bus go to Fiftieth Street?
H: Yes, it does. Step in, please.
G: What's the fare?
H: Seventy-five cents.
G: O.K. Here's a dollar.
H: Can't you read? "Exact change only."
G: Oh, O.K. I have three quarters here. Can you tell me when we get to Fiftieth Street?
H: O.K.
G: Thanks a lot.

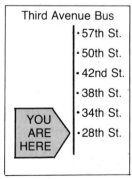

Third Avenue Bus
- 57th St.
- 50th St.
- 42nd St.
- 38th St.
- 34th St.
- 28th St.

YOU ARE HERE

51 Air-sea rescue

This is the WLLN Radio Newsdesk. In Pacific Palisades, a helicopter is trying to rescue a man who has fallen down a cliff. He's lying on a small beach at the foot of the cliff. A Los Angeles Police Department air-sea rescue helicopter has arrived at the scene, and a paramedic has climbed down a ladder to the beach. He's speaking to a doctor on the helicopter by radio.

Paramedic: Hello? Can you hear me, doctor?
Doctor: Yes, I can hear you clearly. Is he unconscious?
Paramedic: No, he's conscious, but he looks pretty bad.
Doctor: O.K. Ask him if he can move
Paramedic: Can you move?
Man: No, I . . . I . . .
Doctor: Ask him if he's in pain.
Paramedic: Are you in pain?
Man: Oh, yes . . . I . . . oh!
Doctor: Ask him where it hurts.
Paramedic: Where does it hurt?
Man: It's . . . my back.
Doctor: Uh, oh. Don't move him. I'm coming down.

Bob Atkinson is the editor of the *Daily Sun*. He's sending a young reporter, Lois Gold, to interview the singer Frank Sonata.
"Now I've arranged an interview for four o'clock at his hotel. Ask him lots of questions. You know—ask him if he likes the city. Ask him what his next record will be and when he recorded it, and ask him where. Ask all the usual questions. But don't ask him how old he is, O.K.?"

Practice

Now you are the editor. You're sending a reporter to interview these famous people. Tell him or her what questions to ask.

The President/Pele/Jane Fonda/Mick Jagger

Exercise 1

Ask him if he's married.
Are you married?

1 Ask him if he's a student.
2 Ask him if he has a car.
3 Ask him if he can swim.
4 Ask him if he likes coffee.
5 Ask him if he enjoys learning English.
6 Ask him if he got up early this morning.
7 Ask him if he has been to Brazil.

Exercise 2

Is she bored?
I don't know. You ask her if she's bored.

1 Does she have any sisters?
2 Can he drive?
3 Does he speak French?
4 Does she like watching TV?
5 Did he go out last night?
6 Has she ever met a movie star?
7 Will he be in class tomorrow?

Exercise 3

Ask her where she lives.
Where do you live?

1 Ask her what time she eats breakfast.
2 Ask her who she met yesterday.
3 Ask her what time she got here.
4 Ask her why she's laughing.
5 Ask her how she goes to work.
6 Ask her how far it is to Miami.
7 Ask her how much money she has.

Exercise 4

Where did she buy her watch?
I don't know. You ask her where she bought her watch.

1 Who did he speak to last night?
2 When did they get married?
3 What has she done today?
4 How many children do they have?
5 Why does he have to go to the police station?
6 How old is she?
7 How much did she pay for her car?

52 UFO

Dick and Janet were driving along a quiet country road in Ohio. They were on their way to Cincinnati. It was almost midnight.

Janet: Dick, look over there. There's something in the sky. What is it?
Dick: I don't know what it is. It's probably a plane.
Janet: I don't think so. It's too big—and too bright.
Dick: You've seen too many movies, Janet. Oh, no!
Janet: What's the matter?
Dick: The engine's just died.
Janet: What's happened to it?
Dick: Well, I don't know what's happened. We'll have to find a garage.
Janet: There's one in the next town.
Dick: Great, but I don't know if it's open. It's really late.

Suddenly there was a loud noise, and a big, bright silver object flew low over their car. It stopped in mid-air, turned around, and flew back over their car. Then it went straight up into the sky and disappeared.

Janet: Wow! What was that?
Dick: Huh? Don't ask me. I have no idea what it was.
Janet: Whew! Let's go.
Dick: We can't. The car won't start.
Janet: Try it again.
Dick: That's strange. It's O.K. now. I wonder why it wasn't working.
Janet: Do you think it was a UFO?
Dick: I don't know. I really don't. We should call the police.
Janet: Do you think they'll believe us?

Exercise 1

Where did it come from? (They don't know.)
They don't know where it came from.

1 What was it? (He has no idea.)
2 Why wasn't the car working? (They wonder.)
3 Where did the object go? (She doesn't know.)
4 What will the police say? (They have no idea.)

Exercise 2

Was it a UFO? (He has no idea.)
He has no idea if it was a UFO.

1 Did it come from another planet? (She wonders.)
2 Is the garage open? (He doesn't know.)
3 Was it a dream? (We don't know.)
4 Will the police believe them? (She has no idea.)

THE SAN DIEGO DAILY SUN

Vol. LXVII   No. 18

Tuesday, February 18

35 cents

SUPERTANKER COLLISION
DRAMA CONTINUES

Slick endangers tourist and fishing industries

A giant oil slick is threatening marine life and local beaches. Several government agencies are working to prevent the loss of millions of dollars to local hotels and the fishing business. Environmental groups have charged that the government is moving too slowly to fight the danger.

The oil slick is the result of a disaster at sea. There was a collision on Monday, about ten miles off the California coast, between the S.S. *Titan*, which is one of the biggest oil tankers in the world, and a Nigerian cargo ship. The collision happened in a thick fog late Monday night and damaged the tanker's engines. It drifted onto rocks and broke in half. The tanker was carrying 1,000,000 tons of crude oil, which formed a giant oil slick on the ocean. The slick is moving slowly toward the coast around San Diego. Helicopters rescued both crews, and nobody died in the collision.

Dozens of small boats, which are carrying straw and detergent, are racing to the scene.

WEATHER

A departing low pressure system will leave mostly sunny skies in the San Diego area today. The temperature will be seasonably cool with a high of 65° to 69°F and westerly winds at 10 to 20 miles per hour. Tonight will be increasingly cloudy, and the temperature will drop into the low 40s or high 30s. Tomorrow will be cloudy and cool with a 30% chance of showers near the coast and light winds.

Where's My House?

Ms. Pat Laine, who lives in Oceanside Cliffs between San Diego and Los Angeles, went home from work last night but couldn't find her house. Ms. Laine's home at 327 Seacrest Drive was near the edge of a cliff, but during the afternoon it fell into the ocean. Recent rains have weakened the cliff, and more houses might fall into the ocean. Local residents are spending the night in a school. The police have warned people not to go back to their homes.

Surprise for a Thief

Somewhere in the San Diego area a thief is in for a big surprise today. Last night someone stole a van which was parked on La Jolla Avenue. The van belonged to the San Diego Zoo. In the back of the van were two boxes. They contained poisonous snakes. The van was on its way from the airport to the zoo. The thief took the van while the driver was in a store buying cigarettes.

54 A mugging

1

One night Sara Garcia, an elderly widow, was walking down a dark street in Philadelphia. She was carrying her purse in one hand and a shopping bag in the other. There was nobody else on the street except two young men. They were standing in a dark doorway. One of them was very tall with light hair. The other was short and fat with a beard and mustache.

2

The two men waited for a few moments and then ran quickly and quietly toward Mrs. Garcia. The tall man held her from behind while the other one tried to snatch her purse.

3

Suddenly, Mrs. Garcia threw the tall one over her shoulder. He crashed into the other man, and they both landed on the ground. Without speaking, Mrs. Garcia hit both of them on the head with her purse and walked calmly away.

4

The two surprised young men were still sitting on the ground when Mrs. Garcia crossed the street toward a door with a bright sign above it. Mrs. Garcia paused, turned around, smiled at them, and walked into the Philadelphia Judo Club.

Exercise

Write the story below. The words will help you.

| 5 | 6 | 7 | 8 |

5

Last night, Louis Karpinski/middle-aged widower/street in Kansas City. He/briefcase/umbrella. There/nobody else/two men. They/side street. One/big/dark hair. The other/thin/bald head.

6

They/few seconds and/walk/slowly/silently/Mr. Karpinski. The big man/hold/behind. The thin one/try/steal/Mr. Karpinski/briefcase.

7

Suddenly, Mr. Karpinski/big one/shoulder. He/collide with/thin one. They/land/pavement. Mr. Karpinski/hit/umbrella and/walk/quickly away.

8

The two astonished men sit/ground. Mr. Karpinski/cross/street toward/door/painted sign. Mr. Karpinski/stop/turn/laugh/walk into/Kansas City Karate Club.

55 An important visitor

The Middleburg Airport is full of people. They're waiting for an important visitor—the president's wife, the First Lady. They're expecting her to arrive soon. She's going to attend the opening of a new rehabilitation center for alcoholics. The Mayor of Middleburg is waiting for the First Lady too. His administrative assistant is telling him the plans for the day.

She'll be here soon. We'll wait until the plane is on the ground.

1 When the plane lands, the band will start playing.
2 Your son will give her some flowers when she gets off the plane.
3 You'll make a speech before she leaves the airport.
4 As soon as she arrives at the rehabilitation center the people will begin cheering.
5 After she attends the opening, we'll go to the Purefoy Hotel.
6 When she gets to the hotel, we'll have lunch.
7 After we have lunch, she'll make a speech for your reelection.
8 Before she leaves Middleburg, you'll give her a present as a souvenir of her visit.

Exercise 1

When/see her/say, "Hello."
When I see her I'll say, "Hello."

1 When/see a service station/get some gas.
2 After/have breakfast/brush my teeth.
3 As soon as/wake up/get up.
4 Before/go to bed/turn off the TV.

Exercise 2

Write long answers:
What'll happen when the plane lands?
Who'll make a speech before she leaves the airport?
When will the people begin cheering?
What'll they do after she attends the opening?

Exercise 3

Write answers:
What'll you do when you get home tonight?
What'll you do after you have dinner?
What'll you do before you go to bed?
What'll you do as soon as you get up?

56 General Hospital

Maternity Ward

Mr. Diaz is in the maternity ward. His wife's going to have a baby.

Nurse: Hello. You're Mr. Diaz, aren't you? Have you been waiting long?
Mr. Diaz: Not really. Is there any news?
Nurse: Not yet. We'll tell you as soon as there is. Have you thought of any names for the baby?
Mr. Diaz: Oh, yes. If it's a girl, we'll call her Lucia, and if it's a boy we'll call him Francisco.

Operating Room

David Foster has had a serious accident. His wife's outside the operating room now.

Doctor: Mrs. Foster? I'm Dr. Yamamura.
Mrs. Foster: Oh, doctor, how is he?
Doctor: Well, I'm afraid we'll have to operate.
Mrs. Foster: Oh, no! He's always been afraid of operations.
Doctor: Don't worry. If we operate now, he'll be all right.
Mrs. Foster: Oh, doctor, do you really have to?
Doctor: I'm afraid so. He's lost a lot of blood. If we don't operate, he'll die!

Ward Ten

Ms. Wright has just arrived at the hospital. She's going to have a minor operation tomorrow.

Nurse: This is your bed, Ms. Wright.
Ms. Wright: Oh, thank you, nurse.
Nurse: Now, get undressed and get into bed. There's a buzzer on the night table. If you press the button, someone will come right away.
Ms. Wright: Oh, I'm sure I won't need anything.
Nurse: Well, don't forget—if you need anything, just press the buzzer.

Emergency Room

Doctor: Oh! How did this happen?
Mother: He was playing soldier, and he put the pot over his head. Now it's stuck!
Doctor: Have you tried to get it off?
Mother: No, I'm afraid of hurting him.
Doctor: Yes, if we pull too hard, we'll hurt him.
Mother: What are you going to do?
Doctor: Well, if I don't get it off, he won't be able to eat!
Mother: Oh, no!
Doctor: I'm only joking. If I put some soap on his head, it'll come off easily.

Exercise

We/operate/he/be all right.
If we operate, he'll be all right.

Write sentences using:
You/take these pills/feel better.
You/eat too much/get sick.
He/press the buzzer/nurse/come.
You/not take the medicine/not feel better.
You/not eat/not get well.
She/have a boy/call/Shawn.

57 At the races

KENTUCKY DERBY

Key to Form

P P S L 0 W

This list shows the results of the horse's six previous races.

W win (first)
P place (second) ⎫
S show (third)   ⎬ "in the money"
4 fourth   ⎭
0 unplaced
L last

Key to odds

3-1

If you bet one dollar and the horse wins, you'll win three dollars.

KENTUCKY DERBY

Number	Name	Odds	Form					
1	Black Beauty	20-1	0	0	4	0	0	S
2	Prussian Prince	3-1	S	4	S	S	W	0
3	Concorde	4-1	W	P	0	0	P	S
4	White Rum	1-1	W	W	W	W	W	W
5	Carolina Moon	14-1	P	0	0	0	4	S
6	Cash Register	2-1	S	P	P	S	0	W
7	Dancing Loon	33-1	0	0	0	0	0	0
8	Sophisticated Lady	25-1	0	0	4	0	0	0
9	Native Speaker	100-1	L	L	L	0	L	L
10	Sylvester Stallion	10-1	4	4	P	0	0	W
11	Tricky Dicky	66-1	0	L	0	0	L	0
12	Trigger	50-1	0	L	0	0	0	4

Horse racing is a popular sport all over the world. It is also one of the oldest sports. The British developed the modern version of horse racing, and they often call it the "sport of kings." But there is more horse racing in other countries. In the United States, there are more than 40,000 races every year, and about 40,000,000 people go to these races. The second country is Australia, and the third is Argentina. Some of the prizes are worth thousands of dollars, and some of the horses are worth millions. People bet on the horses. If they are lucky, they can win lots of money. Some people spend a lot of time studying the form of the horses. Others just guess. Look at the list of horses for the Kentucky Derby. Try to choose the winner.

Ask each other these questions

Which horse did you choose?
What number is it? What are the odds?
Why did you choose it? Has it won before?
How much are you going to bet?
If you win, how much will you get?

"It's a beautiful day here at Churchill Downs. The horses are ready for today's big race, the year's biggest race—the Kentucky Derby. For more than a hundred years, the Kentucky Derby has been the World Series, the Davis Cup, the Super Bowl of horse racing! The horses are at the starting gate. And they're off. They're racing toward the first turn, and Native Speaker is in the lead. Concorde's second, and Sophisticated Lady is third. Now they're coming to the turn into the backstretch. Native Speaker is falling behind, and Concorde takes the lead. White Rum, the favorite, is in the back. In the backstretch, Cash Register is passing Concorde, and Sylvester Stallion moves into third place, then Prussian Prince, then Tricky Dicky. Now they're coming around the far turn, and it looks very close. White Rum is moving up fast, and the crowd here is cheering wildly. Now they've turned into the homestretch. All the horses are in a line, and I can't see which one's in front. It's going to be very, very close. Yes, it's a photo finish! What a race! But we'll have to wait for the results."

58 On the road

Anne: Lee! You can't park here. There's a fire hydrant.

Lee: Oh, we'll be back in a few minutes. It's O.K.

Anne: Oh, no, it isn't. You'll get a parking ticket if you leave it here.

Lee: No, I won't. It's five-thirty. All the traffic officers have gone home.

Anne: Oh, Lee . . .

Lee: Yes?

Traffic Officer: Is this your car, buddy?

a fire hydrant
a bus stop
a crosswalk
a no-parking sign

Patrol Officer: May I see your license?

Lee: Sure. Oh, I've left it at home.

P.O.: In that case, you'll have to come with us to the station.

Lee: But . . . but why?

P.O.: You were speeding, buddy.

Lee: But I was only doing 35!

P.O.: There's a 30 mile-an-hour speed limit. It's a residential section.

Lee: Really? I didn't see the sign.

P.O.: We've been following you.

Lee: So you were doing 35 too.

P.O.: No. We were doing 60 miles an hour—and we couldn't catch you!

35 mph/
  30 mph speed limit/
  residential section

55 mph/
  45 mph speed limit/
  business zone

30 mph/
  25 mph speed limit/
  school zone

60 mph/
  55 mph speed limit/
  federal law

Woman: Hello. Turnpike Service Station.

Lee: Hi. I don't know if you can help me. My car's broken down.

Woman: We have 24-hour service. Where are you?

Lee: I'm on US 31, just south of Hopeville. My car's just past the Red Bird Cafe. It's a gray Mustang.

Woman: Do you know what's wrong with it?

Lee: I have no idea. But it won't start.

Woman: I'll send a mechanic out to you. He'll be there in about ten minutes.

US 31/south
I 95/north
US 66/west
I 65/east

Mechanic: It's nothing serious. You've just run out of gas.

Lee: Oh. Can you tow me back to the service station?

Mechanic: That's not necessary. I have a spare can of gas with me.

Lee: Do I pay you now or do I pay at the service station?

Mechanic: You can pay me now.

Lee: Will you take a credit card? I've run out of cash too.

Mechanic: Yes, that's O.K.

Lee: Hold it. I can't find my wallet!

You've run out of gas/a
  spare can of gas

You don't have enough
  oil/some cans of oil

The radiator's
  empty/some water

The battery's dead/a
  new battery

59 A trip to Mexico City

167 Woodley Road
Cleveland, Ohio 44101
October 1

Pensión San José
Hamburgo 243
Zona Rosa
México 5, D.F.

Dear Sir or Madam:

I would like to reserve a single room with private bath for 3 nights from Friday, October 20th to Monday, October 23rd. Please let me know if I should send a deposit. Also, please confirm my reservation by return mail. Thank you.

Sincerely Yours,

John Carter

Pension San José
Hamburgo 243, Zona Rosa, México 5, D. F.

October 5, 1983

Mr. John Carter
167 Woodley Road
Cleveland, OH 44101
U.S.A.

Dear Mr. Carter:

Thank you for your letter of October 1. This will confirm your reservation for the nights of October 20, 21, and 22. It is not necessary to send a deposit. We look forward to seeing you and hope that you will enjoy your stay with us.

Yours sincerely,

Simon Almendares
Simon Almendares
Reservations Manager

TELEGRAMA INTERNACIONAL

SECRETARIA DE COMUNICACIONES Y TRANSPORTES
DIRECCION GENERAL DE TELECOMUNICACIONES

SERVICIO TELEGRAFICO CON TODO EL MUNDO

MARY COLLIER
AMBERES 39
ZONA ROSA
MEXICO 5, D.F.

ARRIVING FRIDAY OCTOBER 20 6:30 PM PAN AM 301 FROM DALLAS.
LOVE JOHN

Exercise 1

Now write a letter to reserve a room at the Seagate Hotel, 1210 Ocean View Road, Delray Beach, Florida.

Exercise 2

Now write a reply from the hotel.
Begin *Dear Mr. . . . , Ms. . . . , Mrs. . . . ,* or *Miss . . .*

Exercise 3

Now write a telegram to a friend.
Tell him when you'll get home.
Use twelve words or less.

60 Emergency—Dial 911

Operator: Police Operator 366.
Caller: I've just seen two cars crash into an armored truck. I think it's a robbery.
Operator: Where?
Caller: Just outside the factory gates.
Operator: Which factory?
Caller: McManus Forge Company on Old Selma Road.

The first police car got to the factory three minutes later, but it was too late. The robbers had gone. They had knocked out one of the security guards and shot the other. They were both lying on the ground near the armored truck. The thieves had taken all the payroll for the factory. The police called an ambulance for the guards and questioned three people who had seen the robbery.

Operator: Police Operator 217.
Caller: I want to report a fire.
Operator: Where is it?
Caller: The Pexico Service Station on Hudson Street. Come quickly!
Operator: Yes. I'll call the Fire Department. A fire engine will be there in a few minutes.

The fire engine got to the service station just in time. The candy and cigarette store in the station was burning. Fortunately the fire hadn't reached the gas pumps and hadn't spread to the neighboring houses. The fire fighters were able to put it out quickly. The fire had started in the office. Someone had thrown a lighted cigarette into a wastepaper basket.

Operator: Police Operator 577.
Caller: There's a boy in the river. I don't think he can swim. I can see him from my window.
Operator: In the river? Where?
Caller: Oh, I'm sorry. Near Key Bridge. The Washington end of the bridge.
Operator: I'll send a paramedic ambulance right away.

When the paramedic ambulance got there, the boy was lying on the ground. A police officer had seen the boy in the river and had dived in and rescued him. The boy was all right. The police officer had given him artificial respiration. The ambulance took the boy and the police officer to the hospital.

Exercise

3:00: The police arrived. 2:55: The robbers went.
When the police arrived, the robbers had gone.

7:00: He got to the airport. 6:50: The plane took off.
• • • .

9:05: The student came to school. 9:00: The class started.
• • • .

4:50: The helicopter arrived. 4:15: The boat sank.
• • • .

11:20: She went out. 11:18: The rain stopped.
• • • .

Readers' Letters

Oh, no! . . . Have you ever had an embarrassing experience? Who hasn't? Last week we asked our readers to tell us about their embarrassing experiences. We received hundreds of letters! Here is a selection.

A smart teacher!

. . . My most embarrassing experience happened when I had just finished college. I had just started teaching at a high school in Denver. One morning my alarm clock didn't go off — I had forgotten to set it. I woke up at 8:00, and school started at 8:30. Quickly I washed, shaved, dressed, jumped in my car, and drove to school. When I got there, classes had already started. I didn't go to the office or the teacher's room but went straight into my first period class. After two or three minutes the students started laughing, and I couldn't understand why. Suddenly I looked down and understood. I had put on one black shoe and one brown shoe!
Stanley Morris, Boulder, CO

Hand in hand

The most embarrassing experience I've ever had happened two years ago. My wife and I had driven into New York to do some shopping. The streets were very crowded, and we were holding hands. Suddenly my wife saw a dress that she liked in a store window and stopped. I started looking at some radios in the next window. After a minute or two I reached for my wife's hand. There was a loud scream, and a woman slapped my face. I hadn't taken my wife's hand — I had taken the hand of a complete stranger!
Gary Hall, Paramus, NJ

A parking problem

My husband and I had decided to buy a new house, and I'd made an appointment to see our bank manager. I'd never met him before, and I was a little nervous. I drove into town, and I was lucky enough to find a parking space outside the bank. I'd just started backing into the space when another car drove into it. I was furious! I opened my window and shouted at the other driver. He ignored me and walked away. It took me twenty minutes to find another space. As soon as I had parked the car, I rushed back to the bank. I was ten minutes late for my appointment. I went to the manager's office, knocked, and walked in. The manager was sitting behind his desk. He was the man who had taken my parking space!
Margaret Larcade, San Antonio, TX

Why don't you write and tell us about your most embarrassing experience?

62 A ghost story

Doug and Kay are staying in an old house on Cape Cod. It belongs to Doug's uncle, and they've borrowed it for the weekend. It's Friday night. They arrived an hour or two ago, and they're sitting in front of a fire in the living room downstairs. It's January, and a cold wind is blowing outside.

Kay: Oh, Doug, this house is fantastic! I love old houses.
Doug: There's a ghost here, you know.
Kay: What? Don't be silly. Are you trying to scare me?
Doug: No, really. I've been coming here for years. We used to stay here when I was a kid. I saw the ghost myself once.
Kay: Very funny, Doug. I don't believe in ghosts.
Doug: You don't? Well, I do.
Kay: Where did you see the ghost?
Doug: Upstairs—in the bedroom.
Kay: Ha, ha. Did it have a white sheet over its head?
Doug: No, no. It was just an ordinary ghost. He was wearing clothes from the 1800s.
Kay: He? Who?
Doug: The ghost. I'll tell you about it. I'd been out riding a bicycle all day and I was really tired, so I went to bed early.
Kay: Had you been drinking?
Doug: No, no.
Kay: Well, go on. What happened?
Doug: I'd been in bed for two or three hours . . .
Kay: How did you know that it was a few hours?
Doug: There's an old grandfather clock in the bedroom. You'll see it when we go upstairs. Anyway, the man was standing beside it.
Kay: What man?
Doug: The ghost, of course.
Kay: What did you do?
Doug: Nothing.
Kay: What did he say?
Doug: Nothing. He just stared at me.
Kay: How did he get into the room? Hadn't you locked the door?
Doug: Yes, I had—and the window too. It was a cold, foggy night like tonight.
Kay: Was there a fireplace?
Doug: Yes, but it was too small for a man to get down. Anyway, there'd been a fire.
Kay: What did you do?
Doug: I sat up and stared back at him. I was too shocked to move.
Kay: Well? What happened?
Doug: I don't know how long we'd been staring at each other, when suddenly I panicked and shouted—and he disappeared.
Kay: I don't believe it.
Doug: I didn't believe it myself—at the time—but when I told some people who live around here, they believed me. Some of them had seen the ghost themselves. They could even describe him. If you ask them, they'll tell you.
Kay: Doug, put some more wood on the fire. I'm going to sleep right here tonight.

Exercise

Do you believe in ghosts? Have you ever seen one?
Can you tell a ghost story?

63 Buying a present

In a record store

Liz: Do you have *Disco King*, please?

Salesclerk: Who's it by?

Liz: Soul Sensation. It's their latest single. It's just made the charts. It's number nine this week.

Salesclerk: Let's see . . . just a minute. Yes. Here you are.

Liz: Oh, thanks. And do you have the new album by the Rats?

Salesclerk: *Teenage Revolution?* Oh, yes. We have that. It's a terrific album. You'll love it.

Liz: Oh, it's not for me. It's for my grandmother. It's a birthday present.

THIS WEEK'S TOP TEN HITS
1 Love Me, Baby
  Lorna Winter
2 Teenage Revolution
  The Rats
3 You're My Lady
  Phil Crockett
4 The Golden City
  Fantasy
5 Happy Summer Days
  Danny Kleen
6 Spaceship
  Computer
7 Midnight Blues
  Mervyn Thomas
8 Jamaica Rhythm
  The Brothers
9 Disco King
  Soul Sensation
10 The Breakthrough
  Streamline Express

In a jewelry store

Harry: I'm trying to find a Christmas present for my wife.

Salesclerk: All right. What exactly are you looking for?

Harry: I'm not sure, really. Maybe you can help me.

Salesclerk: Sure. I'll show you some bracelets.

Harry: No, I bought a bracelet for our anniversary.

Salesclerk: Maybe a ring, then. These rings are made of gold.

Harry: Yes, I like that one. What kind of stone is that?

Salesclerk: It's a diamond. And it's only $5,000!

Harry: Oh. Well, maybe you could show me some earrings, then.

bracelet
pin
chain
ring
necklace
earrings

gold (Au)
silver (Ag)
platinum (Pt)
copper (Cu)

diamond
ruby
emerald
sapphire

In a toy store

Mrs. Silva: Hello. Maybe you could advise me.

Salesclerk: Yes, of course.

Mrs. Silva: I'm looking for a toy for my nephew.

Salesclerk: O.K. How old is he?

Mrs. Silva: He'll be nine on Saturday.

Salesclerk: Skateboards are still very popular.

Mrs. Silva: Hmm. I don't want him to hurt himself.

Salesclerk: What about a drum set?

Mrs. Silva: I don't think so. His father will be upset if I buy him one of those. Do you have anything educational? You see, he's a very intelligent boy.

Salesclerk: I have the perfect thing! A do-it-yourself computer kit.

nephew
niece
grandson
granddaughter

64 Made in the USA

Brian: I like your radio. Is it new?
Pat: Yes, I bought it last week. It's a Bisonic.
Brian: Bisonic? I've never heard of it. Where was it made?
Pat: I'm not sure. I think it was made in Japan. Let's see. No, I was wrong. It was made in the United States.

Where was your	watch pen pencil shirt dress jacket wallet	made?

Where were your	shoes socks jeans glasses pants	made?

(I think)	it was they were	made in (the U.S.).

I don't know I'm not sure	where	it was they were	made.

Questions

In your house, is there a TV/washing machine/food processor/clock radio/camera/cassette recorder/hair dryer?

Where was it made?

Questions

Cadillacs are made in the United States.

What about Datsuns/Fiats/Mercedes-Benzes/Renaults/Chevrolets/Volvos/Rolls-Royces?

What about Omega watches/Sony TVs/Kodak cameras/Gucci shoes/Braun hair dryers/Honda motorcycles/IBM typewriters/Memorex cassettes?

Questions

A lot of things are made in the United States—cars, planes, TVs, boats.

What things are made in your country/state/town/city?

Questions

The United States imports a lot of things. Coffee is imported from Brazil.

Make sentences using:

wood/Canada
wine/France
oil/Saudi Arabia
bauxite/Jamaica
marmalade/England
bananas/Ecuador

Questions

Milk Wheat Beef Lettuce Corn	is produced on American farms.

Eggs Potatoes Cucumbers Tomatoes Carrots Soybeans	are produced on American farms.

What	is are	produced on farms in your country?

Exercise

Clothes are washed at *a laundromat.*

Movies are shown at • • • .
Newspapers are sold at • • • • .
Cars are repaired at • • • .
Hair is cut at • • • .
Photographs are taken at • • • • .
Bread is sold at • • • .
Checks are cashed at • • • .

studio
bank
supermarket
newsstand
theater
garage
hairstylist's

Quiz

1. The first book was printed in	France	☐	Germany	☐	England	☐
2. IBM computers are made in	Japan	☐	Italy	☐	the USA	☐
3. John F. Kennedy was assassinated in	Dallas	☐	Houston	☐	New York	☐
4. Mount Everest was climbed for the first time in	1953	☐	1980	☐	1892	☐
5. Christopher Columbus was born in	Portugal	☐	Italy	☐	Spain	☐
6. Coffee is exported by	Colombia	☐	Canada	☐	France	☐
7. The Taj Mahal was built in	the 17th century	☐	the 19th century	☐	the 20th century	☐
8. Television was invented by	John Baird	☐	Thomas Edison	☐	Marconi	☐
9. Uranium was discovered in	1944	☐	1932	☐	1789	☐
10. The transistor was invented in	Holland	☐	the USA	☐	Japan	☐

Answers: 1. Germany **2.** the USA **3.** Dallas **4.** 1953 **5.** Italy **6.** Colombia **7.** the 17th century **8.** John Baird **9.** 1789 **10.** the USA.

65 A real bargain

Donna Woo is looking for a new house. She's tired of living in the city, and she wants to live in a quiet town. She's with the real estate agent now.

Real estate agent: Well, Ms. Woo, this is the house that I told you about: 341 Watson Road. The owners are away, but I have the keys.

Donna Woo: Hmm. When was it built?

Agent: It was built in 1926.

Donna: Who built it?

Agent: I'm not really sure. Is it important?

Donna: No, not really. Is that a new roof? It looks new.

Agent: It's pretty new. It was put on two years ago.

Agent: You can see that it's in very good condition. The previous owner was a builder.

Donna: It's really old. I'm worried about the electrical wiring. Has it been rewired?

Agent: Yes, it has.

Donna: Oh? When was it done?

Agent: Five years ago. It's been completely restored. Central heating and air conditioning have been put in, and a garage has been built.

Donna: Oh? When was that done?

Agent: The garage? Last year—I think. It's a very solid house. It's built of brick with a tiled roof.

Donna: What are the services like?

Agent: Hold on. I've got the details here. Let's see. The garbage is picked up Tuesdays and Thursdays.

Donna: I have a little boy in grammar school. Does a school bus pass nearby?

Agent: Yes, right here on Watson Road. The children are picked up at 8 o'clock, and they're brought home by 3:30.

Donna: It's really not expensive. I've seen a lot of similar houses, and they're more expensive.

Agent: Oh, yes. It's a real bargain.

Donna: Are there any plans for this part of town?

Agent: Excuse me? Plans? Well, a new fire department is going to be built about six blocks north of here.

Donna: Anything else?

Agent: Well, a new Interstate highway will be built next year. You'll be able to get to the city in half the time.

Donna: Where exactly will the interstate be built?

Agent: Well, as a matter of fact, it'll be built just down the street. Watson Road has been chosen as the main exit for the town. It'll be interesting. You'll be able to watch the traffic. . .

Donna: Are you crazy? I think I've been wasting my time here.

Exercise

826 Adams Street.
Row house.
Built: 1925
Wood/shingle roof.
Central heating: 1958.
Restored: 1978.

826 Adams Street is a row house. It was built in 1925. It's built of wood with a shingle roof. Central heating was put in in 1958, and it was restored in 1978.

Now write paragraphs about:

2857 Colonial Drive.
Ranch-style house.
Built: 1956
Brick/shingle roof.
Central air conditioning: 1968.
Garage converted into room: 1976.

648 West 68th Street.
Town house.
Built: 1895
Brownstone/flat roof.
Restored: 1953.
Sauna: 1980.

66 The Six O'Clock Report

Good evening, this is Rose Anne Silvernail with the Six O'Clock Report.

Our top story tonight: Alan Wolfe, the great plane robber, has been caught in Costa Rica. He was arrested in a San José nightclub. He is being questioned at police headquarters, and he will probably be sent back here to Baltimore. Two Baltimore Police Department detectives left for Costa Rica earlier today, and they will help the Costa Rican police in their investigation. In 1980 Wolfe was sentenced to forty years in prison for his part in the Great Plane Robbery at Baltimore's Friendship Airport. He escaped from the Maryland State Penitentiary in April. Since then he has been seen in ten different countries.

The wildcat strike at Chesapeake Steel Company in Essex has ended after talks between union leaders and management. The strike began last weekend after a worker had been fired. He had had an argument with a manager. Five hundred men walked out. The worker has been rehired.

Another tragedy in the music world: Jerry Henderson, the lead guitarist of the rock group the Rats, is dead. He was found unconscious in his Fells Point apartment early this morning. Henderson was rushed to the Johns Hopkins University Hospital but doctors were unable to save his life. A number of bottles, which had been found in his apartment, were taken away by the police. A full investigation is planned.

The painting *Iris Morning* by Penoir was stolen last night from the Baltimore Museum of Art. The painting, which is worth over a million dollars, was given to the museum in 1979. It hasn't been found yet, and all airports are being watched. All vans and trucks are being searched. A reward of $15,000 has been offered for information.

Jumbo, the elephant that escaped from the Baltimore zoo this afternoon, has been caught. Jumbo was chased across Druid Hills Park and was finally captured at a hot dog stand near the park's main gate. A tranquilizer gun was used, and Jumbo was loaded onto a truck and was taken back to the zoo. At the zoo, he was examined by the zoo veterinarian. Fortunately, no damage had been done, and Jumbo will be returned to the elephant house tomorrow.

Bart Cobb, the Baltimore Colts quarterback, has been traded to the Chicago Bears. The contract was signed at noon today. The Bears gave the Colts $1,000,000 for Cobb's contract. Cobb, age 23, was signed by the Colts only 2 months ago when he graduated from Alabama College.

Look at this

Someone did it.	*We don't know who did it.* or *It isn't important who did it.* or *We aren't interested in who did it.*	It was done.

(or *We are more interested in what was done than in who did it.*)

Someone does it . . . . It is done.
Someone is doing it . . . . It is being done.
Someone has done it . . . . It has been done.
Someone had done it . . . . It had been done.
Someone will do it . . . . It will be done.

Exercise 1

Someone stole them. *They were stolen.*

Someone has found it.
Someone is watching it.
Someone cleans the windows.
Someone had taken them.
Someone will buy it.
Someone brought it.
Someone has seen it.
Someone is searching them.
Someone had caught it.
Someone will send it.

Exercise 2

Now write the news for today.

REVIEWS

MOVIES

UFO II
Directed by Stephen Spielman
Written by Stephen Spielman
Produced by Stephen Spielman
Composed by
John Williamson

UFO II, which is now being shown at theaters in major cities, is one of the most exciting films I've ever seen. It was filmed in Hollywood last year, but the special effects were made in England. Steve Newman is brilliant as the Army general, but the real stars are the UFO's themselves. It can be seen at neighborhood theaters beginning next week. Don't miss it!

LISA FRANCIS Songs of the City

BOOKS

Atlantic Crossing
Written by Tyrone Fitzpatrick
Published by Ransom House,
$24.95

This book tells the story of Tyrone Fitzpatrick who crossed the Atlantic Ocean alone in a small wooden boat. The boat was built in Ireland and was designed like the boats that were used by Irish fishermen one thousand years ago. Fitzpatrick thinks America was discovered many years before Columbus was born. The design for the boat was taken from old books which had been found in an Irish monastery. The book is beautifully illustrated with many color photographs and maps. The pictures were taken by Fitzpatrick himself during the voyage.

RECORDS

Songs of the City
by Lisa Francis (ALA Records)
Produced by Carmine Dragone

All the songs on this new album were written by Lisa herself, and the album was recorded live during her recent concert tour. She is accompanied by several well-known musicians: Elton Johnson, Pete Vinley, Bernie Hart, and her sister, Melissa. There is a great variety of music on the album—gentle romantic ballads, soul music, and exciting rock songs. The words to all the songs are printed on the back of the cover.

TELEVISION

The Condor Passes
Directed by Paula Simon (PBC)

This documentary, which was first shown at the Cartagena Film Festival, will be aired on Wednesday at 8 on PBC. The condor is now found in only a few remote places in the Andes and the Rockies. In recent years nests have been robbed and eggs have been stolen. Condors are protected by law, but they are threatened with extinction. Paula Simon spent a year making this program. The everyday habits of the condor have been recorded for future generations.

Exercise

Now write a short review of:
a movie that you've seen.
a book that you've read.
a record that you've heard.
a TV program that you've seen.

68 Elvis Presley—Story of a Superstar

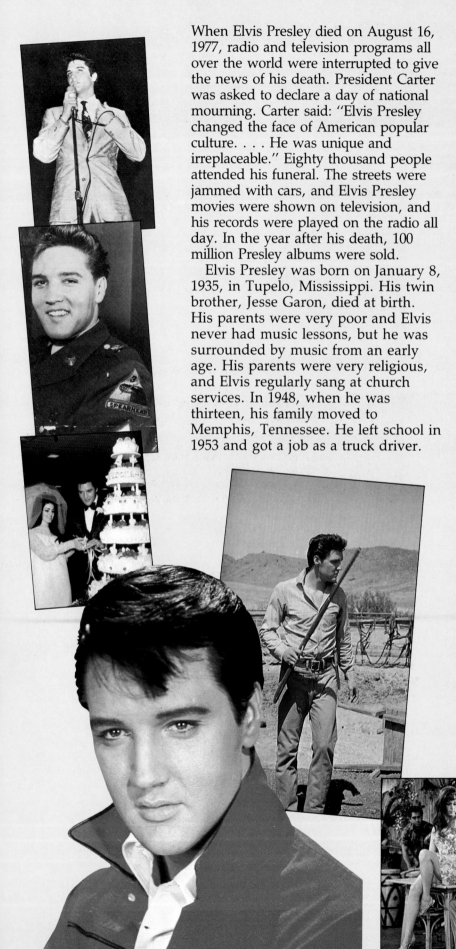

When Elvis Presley died on August 16, 1977, radio and television programs all over the world were interrupted to give the news of his death. President Carter was asked to declare a day of national mourning. Carter said: "Elvis Presley changed the face of American popular culture. . . . He was unique and irreplaceable." Eighty thousand people attended his funeral. The streets were jammed with cars, and Elvis Presley movies were shown on television, and his records were played on the radio all day. In the year after his death, 100 million Presley albums were sold.

Elvis Presley was born on January 8, 1935, in Tupelo, Mississippi. His twin brother, Jesse Garon, died at birth. His parents were very poor and Elvis never had music lessons, but he was surrounded by music from an early age. His parents were very religious, and Elvis regularly sang at church services. In 1948, when he was thirteen, his family moved to Memphis, Tennessee. He left school in 1953 and got a job as a truck driver.

In the summer of 1953 Elvis paid $4 and recorded two songs for his mother's birthday at Sam Phillips's Sun Records studio. Sam Phillips heard Elvis and asked him to record *That's All Right* in July 1954. 20,000 copies were sold, mainly in and around Memphis. He made five more records for Sun, and in July 1955 he met Colonel Tom Parker, who became his manager in November. Parker sold Elvis's contract to RCA Records. Sun Records got $35,000 and Elvis got $5,000. With the money he bought a pink Cadillac for his mother. On January 10, 1956, Elvis recorded *Heartbreak Hotel*, and a million copies were sold. In the next fourteen months he made another fourteen records, and they were all big hits. In 1956 he also made his first movie in Hollywood.

In March 1958, Elvis had to join the army. When his hair was cut thousands of women cried. He spent the next two years in Germany, where he met Priscilla Beaulieu, who became his wife eight years later on May 1, 1967. In 1960 he left the army and went to Hollywood where he made several movies during the next few years.

By 1968 many people had become tired of Elvis. He hadn't performed live since 1960. But he recorded a new album, *From Elvis in Memphis*, and appeared in a TV special. He became popular again, and went to Las Vegas, where he was paid $750,000 for four weeks. In 1972 his wife left him, and they were divorced in October 1973. He died of a heart attack. He had been working too hard and eating and drinking too much for several years. He left all his money to his only daughter, Lisa Marie Presley. She became one of the richest people in the world when she was only nine years old.

69 If I had enough money . . .

Andy

I have $3,000. I'm going to look at the car. If I like it, I'll buy it.

How much is the car?
Does he have enough money?
Is he going to look at the car?
Will he buy it?
What will he do if he likes it?

For Sale: Ford Mustang. Original owner. Very good condition. $3,000. Call 684-6073 after 5.

Barbara

That's a nice car, but I don't have enough money. If I had enough money, I'd buy it!

Does she like the car?
Does she have enough money?
Will she buy the car? Why not?
What would she do if she had enough money?

Chris

I've worked for an oil company for ten years. I have a B.S. in engineering. I have the qualifications. I'm going to apply for the job.
If they offer me the job, I'll definitely take it.

Does he have experience?
Does he have a B.S.?
Is he going to apply?
What will he do if they offer him the job?

Wanted: Engineer. Important offshore oil company. Qualifications: Bachelor of Science and five years' experience in similar work. Send resume to Box 305, New Orleans, LA 70113

Dave

I like that job, but I can't apply for it. I don't have the qualifications.
If I had the qualifications, I'd apply for it.

Does he like the job?
Can he apply?
Why not?
What would he do if he had the qualifications?

Floyd

I'm a mechanic, and I know a lot about cars. I have a current driver's license and enough money. If they ask me, I'll go with them.

What's his job?
How much does he know about cars?
Does he have a current driver's license?
Does he have enough money?
What'll he do if they ask him to go with them?

Personal: Two members needed for overland sub-arctic expedition from Burlington, Vermont, to Nome, Alaska, by Winnebago camper. Applicants must have current driver's license, knowledge of mechanics, and minimum $2,000 for expenses. Write Dick York, Box 96A, Winooski, VT 05679

Tom

I have $2,000 and a current driver's license.
But I know very little about cars.
If I knew something about cars I'd go with them.

Does he have a driver's license?
What about money?
How much does he know about cars?
What would he do if he knew enough about cars?

Jessica

I am a native speaker of English.
I can read and write Spanish.
I'll apply for the job.
If I get it, I'll have to move to New Jersey.

What languages can she read and write?
What languages does she need?
Will she apply?
What'll she have to do if she gets the job?

Wanted: Bilingual secretary for new office in New Jersey. The applicant must be a native speaker of English and must be able to read and write Spanish. Send resume to Texxo Corp. Personnel Department, Princeton, NJ 08540

Helen

I am a native speaker of English, but I can't read or write Spanish.
If I could read and write Spanish, I would apply for the job.

Can she read and write Spanish?
Does she need Spanish?
Can she apply? Why not?
What would she do if she could read and write Spanish?

Darlene

I'm 19 and I'm interested in the job.
I'll get more information if I call.
If the salary's good, I'll apply.

How old is she?
Is she too old?
What'll happen if she calls?
Will she apply?

Wanted: Beginning computer programmer. Opportunity to learn and work. Applicants must be over 18. For more information call (212) 417-0204 from 9 to 5 weekdays.

Jack

I'm interested in the job, but I'm too young. I'm only 17.
If I were older, I'd apply.

Is he over 18 or under 18?
Is he going to apply?
Why not?
What would he do if he were older?

If	I	had enough money,	I	'd	buy that car.
	you	were rich	you	would	travel.
	we		we		etc.
	they		they		
	he		he		
	she		she		

70 In a restaurant

Waiter: Good evening. Two for dinner?

Boris: Yes, that's right.

Waiter: You can leave your coats here. Where would you like to sit?

Boris: Thank you. Where would you like to sit, Natalie?

Waiter: Would you like this table by the window?

Boris: Yes, that's nice. Could we see the menu?

Waiter: Certainly. Here it is. Shall I give you a few minutes to look at it?

Boris: Yes. We'll order in a few minutes.

Boris: Do you want an appetizer?

Natalie: Hmm. I think I'll have a shrimp cocktail. I'm crazy about shrimp. What about you?

Boris: I'm not sure. I can't decide.

Natalie: Oh, if I were you, I'd have the smoked salmon. You always say you like smoked salmon, and you haven't had any for a long time.

Waiter: Are you ready to order now?

Boris: Yes, one shrimp cocktail and one smoked salmon, please.

Waiter: Fine. And the entree?

Boris: Well, we can't decide between the veal and the chicken. What do you recommend?

Waiter: Both are good, but if I were you I'd have the veal. It's the specialty of the house.

Waiter: What would you like with the veal? Maybe some vegetables?

Natalie: Yes. Some zucchini, some carrots, and some boiled potatoes.

Waiter: And a salad?

Natalie: Bring me a mixed salad with the entree, please.

Waiter: All right. Will you want dessert?

Natalie: Can we order that later?

Waiter: Of course.

Waiter: Would you like to see the wine list?

Boris: Yes. We'd like a bottle of red wine.

Waiter: May I suggest something?

Boris: Sure.

Waiter: Why don't you have a carafe of our house wine. It's Chilean. You'll like it.

Boris: That sounds fine. Let's try it.

by the window
by the fireplace
on the side
in the middle

Menu

Appetizers

Shrimp Cocktail	$4.75	Melon (in season)	$2.50
French Onion Soup	$3.50	Smoked Salmon	$4.50
Pate	$3.50	Tomato Juice	$2.00
Avocado with Shrimp	$5.25		

Entrees

Veal (in cream sauce with brandy)	$11.95
Chicken (fried in breadcrumbs)	$8.95
Steak (in red wine sauce with mushrooms)	$10.95
Shrimp Scampi (with tomato and garlic sauce)	$11.95
Roast Beef (with gravy)	$10.95

Salads

Mixed	$3.50	Spinach and Bacon	$2.50

Vegetables

Cauliflower	$2.00	Peas	$1.00
Brussels Sprouts	$2.00	Carrots	$1.00
Green Beans	$1.00	Spinach	$1.50
Potatoes – boiled, baked or french fried	$1.50		

Desserts

Raspberries with cream	$4.95	Ice Cream Parfait	$2.95
Chocolate Mousse	$3.95	Hazelnut Cake	$3.95

Wines

Red		White	
Cabernet Sauvignon		Pinot Chardonnay	
(California)	$18.00	(California)	$18.00
Bardolino (Italy)	$10.00	Soave (Italy)	$9.00
Beaujolais (France)	$12.00	Graves (France)	$13.00
Rioja (Spain)	$9.00	Mosel (Germany)	$10.00

71 Offshore oil

On tonight's edition of "Mississippi Magazine" we'll look at offshore oil in the Gulf of Mexico. Oil was first discovered in the Gulf of Mexico in the 1930s. Since then more oil has been found off the coasts of Florida, Alabama, Mississippi, Louisiana, and Texas. More money is being brought into the state of Mississippi from offshore drilling leases. We aren't going to become very rich, but we must decide how to spend the oil revenue. We took our TV cameras into the streets to ask people their opinion. Our question was : "If you were the governor of Mississippi, what would you do with the money?"

"Well, of course I'm not the governor, but if I were, I'd spend the money on more hospitals and schools. We need more doctors, nurses, and teachers. We don't have enough good teachers. If salaries were higher, we could keep better teachers. And there aren't enough doctors and nurses either because the medical schools are too small. If they were bigger, we would have more doctors and nurses. Money that is spent now on education and health is an investment for the future."

"I think the answer is simple. Taxes are too high in this country, aren't they? I would reduce state taxes. If we reduced taxes, people would have more money. If they had more money, they'd spend more. Industry would have to produce more, so it would need more workers. There would be more jobs, and we would all be richer."

"I'm very worried about inflation. Prices are too high. If I were governor, I'd help low-income families pay their heating and electric bills. I'd encourage farmers to produce more food, more cheaply. I'd bring more industry into the state. If we did that, everybody would benefit, wouldn't they? There's one thing that makes me happy. I'm glad the money stays in Mississippi. The federal government would spend it on more tanks and bombs."

"There's too much crime and violence nowadays. There aren't enough police officers on the streets. I'd give cities money to increase the size of their police forces, and I'd raise their salaries. If we had more police officers, we'd all feel safer. And I'd increase the benefits for senior citizens. I've worked hard all my life, and I should have a reasonable standard of living."

Exercise

If you were governor of your state/President/ Prime Minister of your country, what would you do?

72 What would you do?

Imagine that you are going to a desert island. You can take six things. Which six things would you take? Why?

If you weren't here, where would you like to be? Why?

If you could be somebody else, who would you like to be? Why?

If you had a million dollars, what would you do? Why?

If I were you . . .

I have a headache. *If I were you, I'd* | *take an aspirin.*
| *go for a walk.*
| *take a nap, etc.*

I want to buy a pet. If you were me, what kind of pet would you buy? Why?
I also want to buy a radio/a car/a watch/a camera/an English book.
Give me some advice.

Now advise these people:

I've lost my passport.

I've been bitten by a snake.

I can't sleep at night.

I want to win an Olympic medal.

I've cut myself.

I've just seen an accident.

I need some money, and the banks are closed.

I want to stop smoking.

I want to be a millionaire.

I've been mugged!

I don't know what to wear . . .

I'm going to a wedding, and I don't know what to wear!
I'm going to a funeral/a disco/a football game/
a picnic/Honolulu/the North Pole/a lecture/
the moon.
Give me some advice.

I don't know what to get . . .

It's my mother's birthday tomorrow, and I don't know what to get her.
It's my father's birthday next week. He'll be 47.
It's my brother's birthday next month. He'll be 16.
It's my sister's birthday on Thursday. She'll be 21.
It's my baby brother's birthday tomorrow. He'll be 3.
It's my little sister's birthday on Sunday. She'll be 10.
Give me some advice.

What would you do? What wouldn't you do?

Los Angeles Daily Echo

30¢

MAD KILLER STRIKES AGAIN

Brad Stafford and Saul Goldberg

Downtown Los Angeles was rocked by another car bomb explosion last night. Dr. Jack Martin was killed when he started his car outside General Hospital.

Five doctors have been killed this year by car bombs. Nobody knows why they were killed or who killed them. A warning letter was sent to the *Daily Echo* two days ago.

Detective Leo Lasky has been put in charge of the investigation.

Look at this

It's important to do it. Someone must do it. It must be done.
It's impossible. Nobody can do it. It can't be done.
It was impossible. Nobody could do it. It couldn't be done.
It's possible. Someone might do it. It might be done.

74 Four reports

Scotty Williston is a new reporter for the London office of the *Los Angeles Daily Echo*. Last week several famous people arrived at London Airport, and Scotty was sent to interview them. Nobody told her very much.

Rafael Calderon del Castillo, Secretary-General of the United Nations: "I'm very busy. I have a lot of appointments. I can't say very much. I'm happy to be in London. I enjoyed my visit in January. I'll be here for only twelve hours. I'm going to meet the Prime Minister. I have no other comments."

Scotty's Report
Rafael Calderon del Castillo visited England yesterday. He arrived at 10 a.m., and we asked him to comment on the international situation. He just made a brief statement. He said that he was very busy and that he had a lot of appointments. He said he couldn't say very much, but he said that he was happy to be here and that he had enjoyed his visit in January. He said he would be here for only twelve hours and that he was going to meet the Prime Minister. He said he had no other comments.

Brutus Cray, retired boxer: "I like newspaper reporters, but I don't have time to say much. Just that I'm the greatest. I've always been the greatest, and I always will be the greatest. I can beat anybody in the world! But I don't fight anymore. I have businesses now in Germany, Brazil, and the United States. I can be a champ in business too. I am a champ—a champ forever! Excuse me."

Scotty's Report
Brutus Cray stopped at London Airport on his way from Frankfurt to São Paulo. Brutus was in a hurry. He said he liked newspaper reporters but that he didn't have time to say much. He said that he was the greatest, he had always been the greatest, and he always would be the greatest. He said he could beat anybody in the world—but that he didn't fight anymore. He said that he had businesses now in Germany, Brazil, and the United States and he could be a champ in business too. He also said he would be a champ forever!

Look at this

Maria said, "It's my car." . . . . She said it was her car.
John said, "I like San Francisco." . . He said he liked San Francisco.
Anne said, "I can swim." . . . . She said she could swim.
Paul said, "I thought about you." . . . He said he had thought about me.
Sue said, "I've been to Paris." . . . . . She said she had been to Paris.
Mike said, "I bought it in Miami." . . . He said he had bought it in Miami.
Yoko said, "I'll go to L.A." . . . . She said she would go to L.A.

Exercise

Now write reports on these statements, which were also made to Scotty Williston at London Airport.

Rob Dillon, popular singer
"I'm not staying in England long.
I'm on my way to the United States.
I'm going to record another album.
I've written ten new songs.
I like recording in Detroit.
I made my last album there.
I'll be in Detroit for six weeks."

Reggie Walker, ex-baseball star
"I don't like reporters.
They've written a lot of lies about me.
They destroyed my marriage.
I have a new career.
I'm tired of baseball.
I'll never play baseball again.
I can't say anything more."

75 Oral exams

Jorge: Hey, Marta! Have you finished the exam?
Marta: Yes, I have. Whew!
Jorge: Was it hard?
Marta: Well, yes. It was hard—pretty hard.
Jorge: Did you pass?
Marta: I don't know. Ms. Nadler didn't tell me.
Jorge: What questions did she ask?
Marta: First she asked me what my name was.
Jorge: That was easy, wasn't it?
Marta: Yes, except I couldn't remember! Then she asked me where I came from and how long I'd been studying here at the institute.
Jorge: And what else did she ask?
Marta: She asked when I had begun taking English, and she asked how I would use English in the future.
Jorge: Yes, yes, go on.
Marta: Then she asked me if I liked the institute and if I lived with my parents.
Jorge: Anything else?
Marta: I'm trying to remember, Jorge. Oh, yes! She asked if I spoke any other languages.
Jorge: Is that all?
Marta: Oh, there were a lot of other questions. She asked me what my hobbies were, and she asked me to tell her about them. Then she gave me a picture and asked me to describe it. Then I was asked to read a passage.
Jorge: What did she say at the end?
Marta: Hmm. Let's see. . . . Oh, Yes! She asked me to tell you to go in— right away.

This is the list of questions that the examiner used when she was asking the questions.

Harbridge University
English Language Institute

Oral Examination: Level 1 – B
These questions must not be shown to the student.

- [✓] 1 What's your name?
- [✓] 2 Where are you from?
- [✓] 3 How long have you been studying at the Institute?
- [✓] 4 When did you begin taking English?
- [ ] 5 How will you use English in the future?
- [ ] 6 Do you like the Institute?
- [ ] 7 Do you live with your parents?
- [ ] 8 Do you speak any other languages?
- [ ] 9 What are your hobbies? Tell me about them.
- [ ] 10 Look at this picture. Describe it.
- [ ] 11 Reading passage

Look at this

"Do you like Japanese food?" . . . . (She) asked (him) if (he) liked Japanese food.
"Have you been to Mexico City?" . . . (He) asked (me) if (I) had been to Mexico City.
"Will you go there?" . . . . (They) asked (us) if (we) would go there.
"What's your address?" . . . . (I) asked (them) what (their) address was.
"How did you come to school?" . . . . . (You) asked (her) how (she) had come to school.
"When can you do it?" . . . . (She) asked (me) when (I) could do it.

76 But you said . . .

Travel Agent: Hello. Can I help you?
Marion: I'm interested in your Curaçao vacation package.
I saw your ad in yesterday's paper.
Agent: Oh, yes! The Caribbean! I can recommend it highly.
Marion: Can you tell me a little more about it?
Agent: Of course. It's a terrific package tour. You'll travel
on a regularly scheduled flight. You'll be met at the
airport and taken to your hotel. The hotel is very near the
beach. It has a swimming pool and a great disco. It's a
very modern place—it was built last year. The restaurant
is wonderful, and drinks are cheap in Curaçao. And you
can walk to the blue waters of the Caribbean in two
minutes.
Marion: It sounds terrific! I'd like to make a reservation.
Agent: Just a minute, and I'll get the form to fill out.

Marion made the reservation and paid a deposit. Two
months later she was in Curaçao. But she was
disappointed. When she got home to Chicago, she went to
see the travel agent.

Travel Agent: Oh! It's Marion York. Did you have a good trip?
Marion: No, I certainly did not have a good trip!
Agent: Oh, I'm sorry to hear that. What was wrong?
Marion: Well, when I got to Curaçao I had to spend four
hours at the airport. You said we would be met, but we
weren't. And you said we would be taken to the hotel.
We weren't, and the taxi cost about $25!
Agent: I see. You had a very bad start. But the hotel was
nice, wasn't it?
Marion: No, it was not! You said it was modern. You were
so right—they hadn't finished building it! We couldn't
sleep because the construction workers were working all
night—on our balcony! You said it had a swimming pool,
and it did. But it was empty. And the restaurant! They
served canned tuna fish every night—tuna and rice, tuna
salad, tuna and spaghetti. . . .
Agent: Oh, no!
Marion: You said that the hotel was near the beach. You
said we could walk there in two minutes.
Agent: Couldn't you?
Marion: Sure, but there was one problem. There was an oil
refinery between the hotel and the beach, and it took half
an hour to walk around it.
Agent: Oh, no! I'm really sorry. We didn't know. We really
can't give you a refund, but we can give you a ten
percent discount on your next vacation trip.
Marion: Next vacation trip! I'm spending my next vacation
right here in Chicago!

Exercise

This is an ad for another vacation package tour. Lynn went there.
None of the things the agent said were true.
You said the hotel had three bars and a restaurant, but it didn't.
You said we would love the food, but we didn't.

Write down her other complaints to the travel agent.

77 Having things done

A: I'm sorry I'm late. I couldn't get the car started this morning.
B: Winter's almost here. The engine was probably cold.
A: It needs a complete tune-up, but garages are so expensive nowadays.
B: Can't you do it yourself?
A: Who? Me? I don't know anything about cars.
B: Well then, if I were you, I'd have it tuned up soon. The garage that I use is reasonable. And have the radiator filled with antifreeze. They say it's going to be a cold winter.

radiator/filled with
 antifreeze
brakes/tested
battery/checked
oil/changed
tires/checked

C: Do you know where there's a good dry cleaners?
D: Why don't you go to that self-service place on 8th Avenue? It's so much cheaper.
C: Well, I'm going to a wedding on Saturday, and I want to have my suit cleaned and pressed. I want to look good.
D: Oh, I see. Well, if I were you, I'd go to Martin's Dry Cleaning on Perry Street. I had a suit cleaned there last week. They did a good job.

suit
coat
skirt
dress
pants

a wedding
a party
a dance
a cocktail party

E: Hi! Do you do alterations?
F: Yes, we do. What did you want done?
E: I'd like to have this skirt lengthened. It's too short.
F: Fine. It'll take about two weeks.
E: And at the same time I want to have this dress shortened. It's a little too long.
F: O.K. Would you mind putting on the skirt first? You can change in there.

two weeks
three days
a week
ten days

skirt/dress
pants/jeans
jacket/coat
overcoat/raincoat

G: Hello, I just happened to be passing by. Can I make an appointment to see the eye doctor?
H: Sure. Would next Friday be good? At three o'clock.
G: Oh, yes. That's fine. I want to have my eyes tested. I think I need new glasses. So, Friday at three. Bye.
H: Bye. Oh, be careful. That isn't the door. It's a window.
G: What? Oh, yes, it is a window. Do you see my problem?

eye doctor/eyes tested
doctor/blood pressure
 taken
dentist/a tooth filled
dentist/my teeth
 cleaned

79 The Appointment

Once upon a time, there was a rich Caliph in Baghdad. He was very famous because he was wise and kind. One morning he sent his servant, Abdul, to the market to buy some fruit. As Abdul was walking through the market, he suddenly felt very cold. He knew that somebody was behind him. He turned around and saw a tall man, dressed in black. He couldn't see the man's face, only his eyes. The man was staring at him, and Abdul began to shiver.
"Who are you? What do you want?" Abdul asked.
The man in black didn't reply.
"What's your name?" Abdul asked nervously.
"I . . . am . . . Death," the stranger replied coldly and turned away.

Abdul dropped his basket and ran all the way back to the Caliph's house. He rushed into the Caliph's room.
"Excuse me, master. I have to leave Baghdad immediately," Abdul said.
"But why? What's happened?" the Caliph asked.
"I've just met Death in the market," Abdul replied.
"Are you sure?" said the Caliph.
"Yes, I'm sure. He was dressed in black, and he stared at me. I'm going to my father's house in Samarra. If I go at once, I'll be there before sunset."
The Caliph could see that Abdul was terrified and gave him permission to go to Samarra.

The Caliph was puzzled. He was fond of Abdul, and he was angry because Abdul had been badly frightened by the stranger in the market. He decided to go to the market and investigate. When he found the man in black, he spoke to him angrily.
"Why did you frighten my servant?"
"Who is your servant?" the stranger replied.
"His name is Abdul," answered the Caliph.
"I didn't want to frighten him. I was just surprised to see him in Baghdad."
"Why were you surprised?" the Caliph asked.
"I was surprised because I have an appointment with him—tonight—in Samarra!"

Exercise

"Excuse me, master. I have to leave Baghdad immediately," Abdul said.
Abdul said that he had to leave Baghdad immediately.

Now, change the three conversations into reported speech.

80 The last letter from Mexico City

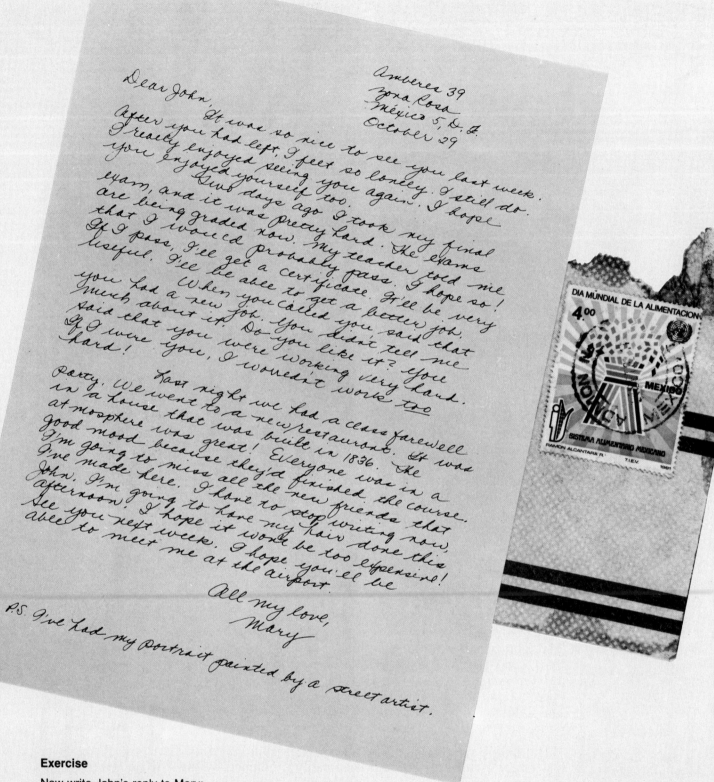

Amberes 39
Zona Rosa
México 5, D.F.
October 29

Dear John,
It was so nice to see you last week.
After you had left, I felt so lonely. I still do.
I really enjoyed seeing you again. I hope
you enjoyed yourself too.
Two days ago I took my final
exam, and it was pretty hard. The exams
are being graded now. My teacher told me
that I would probably pass. I hope so!
If I pass, I'll get a certificate. It'll be very
useful. I'll be able to get a better job.
When you called you said that
you had a new job. You didn't tell me
much about it. Do you like it? You
said that you were working very hard.
If I were you, I wouldn't work too
hard!
Last night we had a class farewell
party. We went to a new restaurant. It was
in a house that was built in 1836. The
atmosphere was great! Everyone was in a
good mood because they'd finished the course.
I'm going to miss all the new friends that
I've made here. I have to stop writing now,
John. I'm going to have my hair done this
afternoon. I hope it won't be too expensive!
See you next week. I hope you'll be
able to meet me at the airport.

All my love,
Mary

P.S. I've had my portrait painted by a street artist.

Exercise

Now write John's reply to Mary:
Write your address and the date/Begin *Dear
Mary*/Tell her that you were pleased to get her
letter/Tell her that you miss her/Ask her if she
passed her exam/Tell her that you hope so/Tell
her that you think she'll be able to get a better
job/Tell her about your new job/Ask her what time
she's arriving/Tell her that you'll be able to meet
her at the airport/Say that you've just bought a
car/Tell her that it's a very old car/Explain that
you're going to have it repainted/Send her all
your love/Sign *John*/Write a P.S. and tell her that
you've had your picture taken.

Vocabulary

This vocabulary contains all the words in the Student's Book, and the number of the unit where they first occur.

A

a 1
able 16
aboard 1
about 5
absolutely 41
accent 45
accessories 50
accident 4
accompany 67
account 43
accounting 2
actress 30
ad 47
administrative
  assistant 10
(in) advance 46
advertisement 53
advertising 2
advice 38
advise 28
afraid 56
afternoon 10
again 6
age (n) 19
agency 53
ago 10
agree 33
ahead 46
air (n) 12
air (v) 67
air conditioning 65
airport 5
air-sea rescue 51
aisle seat 25
alarm 23
alarm clock 61
album 63
alcohol 38
alcoholic 55
alibi 28
all 1
alligator 27
allow 25
all right 4a
almost 19
alone 5
already 25
alterations 77
altitude 25
always 6
am ('m) 1
ambulance 60
amuse 37
an 1a
and 1
angrily 79
animal 12
anniversary 26
another 1a
answer (n) 6
answer (v) 13
antifreeze 77
any 3
anything 10
anyway 21
apartment 17
appetizer 70
applicant 17
application form 22
apply 22
appointment 46
approximately 25
are 1

area 2
argument 30
arm 12
armored truck 60
army 15
around 1
arrange 51
arrest 28
arrive 6
art 44
article 40
artificial respiration 60
as 6
ask 1
aspirin 72
assassinate 64
astonished 54
astronaut 12
at 3
atmosphere 80
attack (v) 39
attend 55
automatic 33
automatic timer 26
available 53
average (n) 4
avocado 70
away 4a
awful 1a

B

baby 6
bachelor's degree 22
back (n) 8
back (adv) 7
backache 9
backstretch 57
bacon 70
bad 6
badly 20
bag 41
bake 70
bakery 64
balcony 76
bald 54
ballad 67
ballet 46
banana 64
band 55
Band-Aid 26
bank 1a
bank officer 43
bank robbery 28
bar 4a
bar (of soap) 9
bar (barroom) 76
bargain 65
baseball 21
basket 79
basketball 20
bass 11
battery 77
bauxite 64
be 1
beach 19
beach house 30
beard 42
beat 74
beautifully 27
become 36
bed 1a
bedroom 29

beef 64
been 1
before 4
begin 4a
beginning 37
believe 13
belong 62
benefit (v) 71
best 3
bet (v) 57
better 3
between 20
big 19
bilingual 69
bill (n) 9
bird 13
birth 68
bit 29
bite (v) 27
black 8
blame 73
bleed 26
blood 37
blood pressure 77
blow 62
blue 9
boardinghouse 42
boarding pass 25
Board of Directors 10
boat 42
boil 70
bomb 71
boo (v) 21
book 43
border 36
bore 37
bored 31
boring 6
born 1a
borrow 43
boss 14
both 3
bother (v) 50
bottle 9
bottom 20
bourbon 29
boutique 50
box 9
boy 30
boyfriend 35
bracelet 63
brakes 77
branch 28
brand new 11
brandy 29
bread 38
bread crumbs 70
break 39
breakfast 42
breathe 12
brick 65
brief 74
briefcase 54
bright 52
brilliant 67
bring 21
bristle 9
brochure 19
brother 37
brownstone 65
brussels sprouts 70
buddy 58
build 64
builder 65

building 15
burn 60
bus 8
business 53
business
  administration 22
bus stop 58
busy 7
but 1
butterfly (swimming
  stroke) 4
buy 10
buzz 25
buzzer 56
by 1a
bye 21

C

cabin 1a
cafeteria 50
cake 70
caliph 79
call 2
calmly 23
camera 64
cameraman 21
camper 69
can (n) 9
can (aux) 2
canal 19
candy 34
canned 76
capsules 9
captain 1a
capture 66
car 8
carafe 70
card 1a
(take) care 21
career 30
careful 26
carefully 12
careless 20
cargo 53
carrot 64
carry 13
case 41
cash (n) 58
cash (v) 18
cassette player 26
cassette recorder 64
cat 13
catch (v) 6
cauliflower 70
cause (v) 23
ceiling 13
Celsius 25
center 4
centimeter 19
central heating 65
century 64
certain 33
certainly 4
certificate 22
chain 63
chair 8
chairman 10
champagne 26
champ 74
chance 53
change (money) 9
change (difference) 31

change (v) 8
channel 26
charge (n) 25
charge (v) 53
charts 63
chase 66
cheap 49
cheaply 71
check (currency) 18
check (bill) 40
check (v) 18
check in 25
checkout counter 78
cheer (v) 21
chef 49
chemical 22
children 3
china 50
chocolate mousse 70
choose 25
church 27
church service 68
cigarette 16
cigarette lighter 25
city 2
class 38
clean (oneself) 26
cleaner (adj) 3
clear (adj) 42
cliff 51
climb (v) 12
clock radio 64
close (to) 23
close-up 21
closing time 28
clothes 3
clothing 50
cloud 12
cloudy 48
club 38
clue 73
coal 71
coast 31
coat 29
cocktail party 77
code 2
coffee 3
coffee shop 13
coin 3
cold 3
collapse 23
collect 2
college 17
collide 54
collision 53
colonel 68
color 8
comb 25
come 1
come on (v) 6
come through 25
comment 74
commercial 15
communications
  expert 15
company 2
comparison 20
competition 4
competitor 4
complain 34
complaint 76
complete 61
complex 4
compose 67